THE Sign

Shawn Boonstra

Pacific Press® Publishing Association
Nampa, Idaho
Oshawa, Ontario, Canada
www.pacificpress.com

Cover design by Fred Knopper
Cover design resources from Photos.com
Inside design by Aaron Troia

Copyright © 2008 by
Pacific Press® Publishing Association
Printed in the United States of America.
All rights reserved.

You can obtain additional copies of this book by calling toll-free
1-800-765-6955 or by visiting http://www.adventistbookcenter.com.

Library of Congress Cataloging-in-Publication Data
Boonstra, Shawn.
The sign / Shawn Boonstra.
p. cm.
ISBN 13: 978-0-8163-2293-0 (paper back)
ISBN 10: 0-8163-2293-7
1. Sabbath. 2. Seventh-day Adventists—Doctrines. I. Title.
BV125.B66 2008
263'.1—dc22

2008030321

08 09 10 11 12 • 5 4 3 2 1

Contents

Chapter One

You Can Have Your Smile Back!

When you go back and read articles from the 1950s predicting the world we would be living in half a century later, you can't help but smile at the naïveté of the authors. It's not that we haven't achieved the kind of technology our grandparents dreamed of. In fact, the raw computing power of my laptop far exceeds the colored lightbulbs and massive dials on the clunky steel boxes that were supposed to be the future of computing. The visionary communicators used by the crew of the Starship *Enterprise* (the original series, of course) seem oversized and inconvenient compared to the cell phone in your pocket. Practically the whole world has been connected to the largest information library in the history of humanity, to the point that third-world villages with little in the way of modern conveniences still seem to have high-speed Internet connections.

No, it isn't the technology our grandparents dreamed of that has become laughable. With the possible exception of moon colonies, we have easily outdone their dreams.

Where we failed is in the leisure department. We were promised that technology would so free up our calendars that people would wonder what to do with all their excess time. The work week was supposed to shrink to thirty—no, *twenty*—hours. It never happened. We invented the labor-saving devices as promised, but we forgot to account for the raw power of human greed and our relentless drive to accomplish things and accumulate possessions. More time on our hands meant more opportunity for relentless activity. Radio psychologist Laura Schlessinger said it well: "How many times have you said, 'I wish I had just a few more hours in the day?' The assumption is that, given more hours, you would accomplish everything you need to with less stress. But there is just as much chance that, given this wish, it would only mean two more hectic hours to live through in a given day. Perhaps we should actually be wishing for a shorter day, in which the crazy pace of our lives is limited to fewer hours."[1]

When extra time suddenly became available, we saw it as an opportunity to do more. Our cell phones and laptops have made it possible to turn a family room or a campground into another office, and for a lot of people, leisure time simply *vanished*.

A little while ago, I was shopping for a new cell phone. My needs are pretty simple: because of a heavy travel schedule, I want an unlocked phone that can be used just about anywhere on earth. When I told the salesman that I needed a phone, he lit up.

"What sorts of features are you looking for?" he asked. "We have phones that can do just about anything! Do you need to be able to sync your calendar with your computer? Send and receive e-mail? Do you use a lot of text messaging?"

"I'm looking for something very specific," I said, "and I don't know if you'll have a phone that can do it."

"Try me!" he replied, obviously proud of the extensive product line in his display case.

"OK," I said, "but it's very specific. It's the number one reason I need a cell phone."

"What is it?"

"It has to be able to make *phone calls*! Do you have one like that?"

He actually looked confused for a moment. I'm guessing I was the only customer he'd seen in months who actually wanted

---

1. Dr. Laura Schlessinger, *The Ten Commandments* (New York: Cliff Street Books, 1998), 95.

a phone to do *less*. We've come to the place that we assume everyone wants to be busy all the time. Of *course* we want access to our e-mail while we're on vacation. Of *course* we want to be able to slap on a Bluetooth headset and attend a business meeting while we're out for a morning walk. Of *course* we never, ever want to be disconnected. Our technology has become a little like an umbilical cord, feeding us a constant stream of information all day long. We fear what would happen if the stream was suddenly cut off—if the power went out and our Internet connection was lost for a few hours. Would we experience withdrawal symptoms, a strange restlessness?

In defiance of yesterday's futurists, the pace of living has become utterly relentless. Ask anyone how life is going, and nine times out of ten, you'll hear him or her say, "I'm *so* busy." We can't unplug, we can't say no, and we can't let go. The results have been unbelievably disastrous for the human family. We have more than those who have gone before, but we've never been so unhappy. The people we deal with every day are irritable and sleep deprived. Heart disease, spurred on by our unmanageable stress levels, has become the number one killer in America (and elsewhere), resulting in another untimely death every thirty-four seconds. In the absence of overworked parents (who are too exhausted to adequately fill the roles of Mom and Dad when they *are* home), many children are left essentially to raise themselves, leading to a whole string of societal problems that would seem foreign to our ancestors.

Life has become very noisy in the twenty-first century. Try this experiment sometime: try to find a place where you can't hear the sounds of human civilization. Unless you are one of those fortunate people who live deep in the wilderness, utterly sequestered from your fellow human beings, you'll find that it has become nearly impossible. If you go camping, somebody with a stereo system will move in next to you. Go for a hike in the woods, and you can hear the sounds of chainsaws or four-wheelers in the distance. Walk on the beach, and you can still hear airplanes passing overhead. There's no escaping the noise.

I should probably admit that I'm as guilty as the next person when it comes to producing noise. When I check into a hotel, one of the first things I do is iron my shirts. But for some reason, I don't like to do it in silence. In spite of the fact that I actually have a chance for quiet contemplation in a place where kids aren't running around and the phone isn't ringing, I usually turn on the TV for background noise! In my car, I rarely drive in silence; the radio is almost always on. Every morning, I go for a long walk—but usually with an iPod piping music straight into my brain through (and here's the irony) noise-blocking headphones!

Now, I'm not an advocate of conspiracy theories, but I have long suspected that the noise and pace of modern life is deliberate. Someone is *trying* to keep us incessantly occupied, because if we stopped the endless cycle of activity for even a few moments, we would discover something amazing: the presence of God.

If you read the Bible, you'll notice that God is not a big fan of noise. There's no question that He has staged some of the noisiest events in history—like the earthquake and trumpet blast that accompanied His visit to Mount Sinai (see Exodus 19:17–20)—but for the most part, God is not to be found in busyness and noise. After a particularly trying experience, the prophet Elijah met God at the same mountain. God sent a number of earth-shattering events: a strong wind, an earthquake, and a fire. But Elijah searched in vain to find His presence in any of them. Finally, God spoke to the prophet in a "still small voice" (1 Kings 19:12). In the book of Psalms, God tells us, "Be still, and know that I am God" (Psalm 46:10).

We have come to think of relentless activity as noble. We wear dark circles under our eyes as a badge of honor, and even though we secretly resent working every spare minute of every day, we actually feel guilty if we spend time doing nothing in particular. Think back to the last time you tried to arrange for some free time. Did you find yourself hesitant to tell people you were actually taking time *off*? Did you excuse your absence by explaining to someone that you were really going to be very busy during that time? Did that first day on the beach make you uneasy?

If so, you wouldn't be alone. Millions of people suffer from *vacation guilt*. It's a condition that stems from the idea that incessant activity is the only socially acceptable state of existence for human beings. We measure a person's worth by how busy he or she is. If we're *not* busy, we feel something is wrong.

Again, I'm as guilty as anyone else. When I go on vacation, it usually takes me about four days to shake the feeling that I should be doing something productive with every waking minute. Sitting on a beach chair with a book makes me feel guilty. If I'm not unflaggingly driving from one vacation destination to the next, always on the move, I feel like I'm not making the most of my time. Like millions of others, I can't seem to turn it off.

It's not healthy. The Bible reveals that unceasing activity was not God's original plan for the human race. He intended for us to balance our drive to *accomplish* with our need to *rest* and bask in His presence. Take a look at this balance as it's presented in the book of Genesis. "Then the LORD God took the man and put him in the garden of Eden to tend and keep it" (Genesis 2:15).

No question about it, we were designed to be fruitful. There's a reason we feel an irresistible urge to create stuff, explore places, and do things. We were created with a divine spark in our hearts to *accomplish*. I imagine Adam waking up on the first day of his life to an eager God waiting to show him the Garden. "Adam, take a look at what I've made for you! It's the perfect environment for the human race. Every tree is good for food, and I've created a river that runs right through the middle of the Garden to make sure you're well taken care of. You should be happy here forever. What do you think?"

And of course, Adam would have been duly impressed. But

notice that God doesn't leave him to spend his days idly strolling through the Garden, plucking fruit off the trees. That might be fun for about two days, but then eternal boredom would set in. Adam and Eve were given something to *do*; they were instructed to tend to the Garden. Created in the very image of the Creator (see Genesis 1:26), they had the desire to create. To this day, we find tremendous satisfaction in making beautiful things.

God's plan went beyond simple gardening, however. "So God created man in His own image; in the image of God He created him; male and female He created them. Then God blessed them, and God said to them, 'Be fruitful and multiply; fill the earth and subdue it; have dominion over the fish of the sea, over the birds of the air, and over every living thing that moves on the earth' " (Genesis 1:27, 28).

Again, I am using my imagination, but I picture God taking Adam and Eve to the edge of Eden one afternoon to show them the rest of the world. "Take a look over the fence," He says, "because I want to show you something important. What do you notice?" God's face is beaming; He knows they're going to like what they see.

Our first parents peek carefully over the hedge, wondering what the Creator has in store for them. Amazed, they report their findings: "Lord, the whole world is *not* a garden!"

"That's right! Your job is to change that. I want you to get out there and name stuff, and explore things, and subdue the whole earth!"

There's something very attractive about a commission like that. It rings true to the human heart. Given the choice between lifting boxes in a warehouse for forty hours a week or conquering the planet, we'll take the latter every time. Given the choice between slaving under fluorescent lights in an office cubicle where no one more than three desks away knows your name or subduing the planet, it's a no-brainer. We were created with the desire to do great things.

God enlisted the human race—in their limited capacity—to

join Him in the joys of creating. We might not be able to speak things into existence as He did, but we were given the mental capacity to take the materials at hand and make something *more* out of them. We can arrange plants into breathtaking oases of beauty. We can manufacture musical instruments and create symphonies that stir the human soul. We can do just about anything we set our minds to. To this day, the aspiration to follow in the footsteps of the Creator is still alive in our hearts. We still have the desire to be *active.*

But creativity and activity are not the only conditions necessary for human happiness. Relentless activity is an unbalanced approach to life, a fact that God made clear all the way back in Eden. "Thus the heavens and the earth, and all the host of them, were finished. And on the seventh day God ended His work which He had done, and He rested on the seventh day from all His work which He had done. Then God blessed the seventh day and sanctified it, because in it He rested from all His work which God had created and made" (Genesis 2:1–3).

After six days of creating, God *took a day off.* Why? Was He so exhausted from the act of creating that He needed a little "downtime" to regain His strength? Of course not. The Bible tells us that unlike human beings, God never gets tired.

> Have you not heard?
> The everlasting God, the LORD,
> The Creator of the ends of the earth,
> Neither faints nor is weary.
> His understanding is unsearchable (Isaiah 40:28).

God didn't take a day off because He needed it, so there must be another reason. He was setting an example for *us.*

When my youngest daughter was two years old, she went through a phase in which she found it exceptionally difficult to stay in bed. Every night, for about a week, she would come out of her room ten minutes after we had put her down for the night. Nothing seemed to persuade that kid to stay in bed, even though we pulled out every parental trick in the book. "Get back in bed!" I commanded. To which she replied, "But I's not tired!"

Finally, remembering a story a preacher friend of mine had told (and to which I am indebted for this illustration), I tried lying on the bed next to her. I closed my eyes and carefully metered my breath, allowing her to hear me "falling asleep." It was only 7:30 P.M., so I wasn't particularly tired. Before long, she took my cue and fell asleep (but not before I fell asleep a few times first!).

Why did I climb on the bed and sleep beside a toddler? To show her the importance of resting. Why did God stop all activity on the seventh day? He didn't need the break, but He knew *we* would, so He set aside one day each week as a day of rest. In the language of the Bible, He "blessed" the day and "sanctified it," which means He set it aside and made it holy. The seventh day is not like the other six days of the week; it has been blessed by God and kept apart for a special purpose. It is sacred.

Nobody was busier than Jesus. With only three and a half years to establish a church and carry out the most important mission any human being has ever been charged with, God in human form still found time for rest. He spent forty days in prayer and contemplation before He got started. With the unrelenting pressure of ministering to human need mounting by the minute, He told His disciples, " 'Come aside by yourselves to a deserted place and rest a while' " (Mark 6:31). He took the time to be in the synagogue every Sabbath (see Luke 4:16). Even with an inconceivably packed schedule and a willingness to be utterly poured out for the good of the human race, Jesus modeled *balance.*

Read the fourth commandment carefully, and you'll find God's thoughtfully planned balance for human beings reiterated:

> "Remember the Sabbath day, to keep it holy. Six days
> you shall labor and do all your work, but the seventh day

is the Sabbath of the LORD your God. In it you sɪ
no work: you, nor your son, nor your daughter, nor ɣ
male servant, nor your female servant, nor your cattɪ
nor your stranger who is within your gates. For in six
days the LORD made the heavens and the earth, the sea,
and all that is in them, and rested the seventh day. Therefore the LORD blessed the Sabbath day and hallowed it"
(Exodus 20:8–11).

Six days are for work. One day is for resting. It's a cycle im-
planted in the human species by the Creator Himself. In a world
overrun with heart attacks, ulcers, and nervous breakdowns, we
ignore it to our peril. When God first created us, He imagined us
with smiles on our faces. Perhaps you've noticed that for most
people, their smiles seem to be missing.

You can have it back.

Chapter Two

A Symbol of Salvation

God's people had been in Egypt for hundreds of years, waiting for the moment when they would return to Canaan to occupy the land that had been promised to their forefather Abraham. The ruler who now sat on the throne didn't remember the blessing that Joseph had been to the nation of Egypt during the famine, and he was worried that if the Hebrews (who already outnumbered the indigenous population) continued to grow, they would soon overrun the Egyptians. The solution seemed obvious—enslave the nation of Israel.

Nothing is as dehumanizing as slavery. A slave's sole reason for existence is to be a source of labor for other people. Apart from this fact, his own life is insignificant. If he should drop dead on the job, he would quickly be replaced by another equally meaningless human being. His own dreams and aspirations count for nothing. If he isn't working, there is no point to his existence.

Of course, we know that God sent Moses to liberate the nation of Israel and restore their dignity as a people. But there is a little-observed detail in the story, prior to the Exodus, that should grab our attention:

> Afterward Moses and Aaron went in and told Pharaoh, "Thus says the LORD God of Israel: 'Let My people go, that they may hold a feast to Me in the wilderness.' "
> And Pharaoh said, "Who is the LORD, that I should

obey His voice to let Israel go? I do not know the LORD, nor will I let Israel go."

So they said, "The God of the Hebrews has met with us. Please, let us go three days' journey into the desert and sacrifice to the LORD our God, lest He fall upon us with pestilence or with the sword."

Then the king of Egypt said to them, "Moses and Aaron, why do you take the people from their work? Get back to your labor." And Pharaoh said, "Look, the people of the land are many now, and you make them rest from their labor!" (Exodus 5:1–5).

Here's an important question: what was the "feast in the wilderness" that God wanted His people to celebrate? The Passover had not yet been established. For that matter, none of the annual feasts of Israel were yet in existence. So what was this "feast" Moses was proposing to Pharaoh?

You find a clue in Pharaoh's protest: "You make them rest from their labor!" In this case, the Hebrew word for "rest" is *shabath,* which is the root word for *shabbath* (Sabbath), the word used in the fourth commandment to describe the seventh day of the week. Both words simply mean "rest." What was Moses proposing? A festival of *rest*!

Now read the psalmist's account of the Exodus, and you'll notice something remarkable:

> He brought out His people with joy,
> His chosen ones with gladness.
> He gave them the lands of the Gentiles,
> And they inherited the labor of the nations,
> That they might observe His statutes
> And keep His laws.
>
> Praise the LORD! (Psalm 105:43–45).

The psalmist indicates that Israel was unable to keep God's laws in the land of Egypt. Pharaoh objected that if Israel went out into the desert to keep their feast, they would be resting from their labor. I'll grant that the evidence is circumstantial, but if you connect the dots, an amazing picture begins to surface. There is a portion of God's law that deals specifically with rest from labor—the Sabbath commandment. And to the best of our knowledge, there was only one "feast" in existence prior to Israel's departure from Egypt—the seventh day Sabbath, sanctified by God at Creation.

When Israel's workload became unbearable and they were sinking under the humiliation of slavery, God ordered them to *rest.* I've always found it fascinating that in the two versions of the Ten Commandments spelled out in the Bible, God gives two different reasons for observing the Sabbath. Here's the version found in Exodus: "For in six days the LORD made heaven and earth, the sea, and all that in them is, and rested the seventh day: wherefore the LORD blessed the sabbath day, and hallowed it" (Exodus 20:11, KJV).

What's the reason for keeping the Sabbath? It's a memorial to God's creative power. It was established at Creation and set apart for holy use. It was "hallowed."

Now look at the reason for the Sabbath given in the second version of the Ten Commandments: " ' "And remember that you were a slave in the land of Egypt, and the LORD your God brought you out from there by a mighty hand and by an outstretched arm; therefore the LORD your God commanded you to keep the Sabbath day" ' " (Deuteronomy 5:15).

I've heard some people suggest that the Bible is inconsistent because of these two different accounts. There is nothing contradictory about them, however. Before human beings rebelled against God, the Sabbath was both a day of rest and a memorial of God's creative power. After we fell into sin, it came to stand for something else: freedom from slavery. In addition to its original significance, it became God's special sign that He had a concrete plan to save us from the misery of sin. We shouldn't look at the Deuteronomy account as an *alternate* reason to celebrate the Sabbath; we should look at it as an *additional* reason to celebrate it. God is busy restoring our world to its original state.

I like to think of the Sabbath as God's warranty plan for a defective planet. I don't know about you, but I've become a little suspicious of claims made by most companies that they intend to guarantee their products. It seems that the moment you pay for something, the promises evaporate. Some years ago, my wife bought some software at a store, and when she got home and opened the box, she found the wrong installation CD inside. We promptly returned to the store to show the clerk the problem, at which point we were told she couldn't help us and we had to contact the manufacturer if we had a problem.

"But we bought this here not half an hour ago!" I protested. "We simply want an exchange or a refund." It wasn't an expensive item; there was perhaps fifteen dollars at stake.

"How do I know you haven't already made a copy of that CD?" the clerk demanded.

I was a little irritated at the suggestion that we were doing something dishonest. "I assure you, we don't *want* this CD. Whether or not I made a copy—and I *didn't*—still doesn't change the fact that you sold us something defective. Perhaps you could exchange this and then contact the company yourself."

I had faith that she would see the value of good customer relations, but what next came out of her mouth dumbfounded me: "It's not my fault you're too stupid to know how this works. It's not my problem." (To be honest, she peppered her response with a few descriptive words which aren't suitable for print.)

Fast-forward a few years. I've just purchased a new cell phone plan with a well-known communications giant. Everything is going well, until I realize—the next day—that my voicemail isn't working. I return to the store and explain the problem to the clerk behind the counter. He can't be less helpful. "You'll have to contact customer service yourself," he tells me. "I can't help you."

"But I just bought the plan the day before yesterday," I say. "Surely you can do *something*. Maybe you could exchange the phone for one that works."

He shakes his head, confirming what I suspect—once you sign the contract, you're essentially on your own. (For the record, I'm happy to report that I did contact customer service, and the representative was not only appalled at what the store clerk had said, she also fixed the problem in less than five minutes.)

The situation with our planet is a little different. It's defective, but it's clearly not the Designer's fault. We corrupted it ourselves, through our rebellion. But in spite of that, God is executing a well-thought-out plan to restore this world to its factory default settings. "I'll take you out of your self-imposed slavery to sin," He says, "even though you sold yourselves into it. And as a reminder that I have the power to *re*-create what I created in the first place, you have the Sabbath."

I've heard a number of preachers say that since Christ died on the cross, the Sabbath has become unnecessary. Why? Supposedly because Old Testament believers were trying to deserve salvation through their works, while New Testament believers are leaning on Christ through faith. This is an unfortunate misunderstanding of the purpose of the Sabbath. In the first place, God set the seventh day aside and blessed it *before* our rebellion against Him, which means He established it quite apart from any human need for salvation. Second, it misunderstands the secondary meaning of the Sabbath—redemption from slavery—as explained by God Himself: " ' "The LORD your God brought you out from there by a mighty hand and by an outstretched arm" ' " (Deuteronomy 5:15).

The nation of Israel was utterly helpless in the land of Egypt, incapable of freeing themselves from slavery. Their *only* hope was an act of God. Before they left, they were instructed to paint their doorposts with the blood of a lamb so that the angel of death would "pass over" their homes—a clear symbol pointing to the redemption from eternal death that the sacrifice of Christ on the cross purchased for those sold into the slavery of sin. There was nothing legalistic or self-aggrandizing about Israel's redemption from slavery. The celebration they held on the far side of the Red Sea after the drowning of the Egyptians wasn't a commemoration of Israel's might in battle; it was a declaration of God's goodness in delivering His people from slavery:

> Then Moses and the children of Israel sang this song to the LORD, and spoke, saying:

> "I will sing to the LORD,
> For He has triumphed gloriously!
> The horse and its rider
> He has thrown into the sea!
> The LORD is my strength and song,
> And He has become my salvation;
> He is my God, and I will praise Him;
> My father's God, and I will exalt Him" (Exodus 15:1, 2).

This passage, which goes on at some length, has come to be known as the "Song of Moses." If you want to see something incredible, look at the song God's redeemed people sing after the second coming of Christ. The book of Revelation describes it:

> And I saw something like a sea of glass mingled with fire, and those who have the victory over the beast, over his image and over his mark and over the number of his name, standing on the sea of glass, having harps of God.
> And they sing the song of Moses, the servant of God, and the song of the Lamb, saying:

"Great and marvelous are Your works,
Lord God Almighty!
Just and true are Your ways,
O King of the saints!" (Revelation 15:2, 3).

Israel and the Christian church sing the same song. That's because we are celebrating the same thing. We have been saved, not by our own ability or power, but by a mighty act of God. When God told the Israelites to go on celebrating the Sabbath in commemoration of their delivery from Egyptian slavery, He wasn't asking them to earn anything. He was telling them to celebrate *His* power, which was, after all, the original purpose of the Sabbath at Creation.

When my wife and I decided to start celebrating the Sabbath, some people suggested we were trying to earn our salvation by doing so. Nothing could be further from the truth. We honor the Sabbath precisely because we *can't* earn our salvation. Salvation is as an act of God, quite apart from anything we might imagine ourselves able to contribute: "For by grace you have been saved through faith, and that not of yourselves; it is the gift of God, not of works, lest anyone should boast. For we are His workmanship, created in Christ Jesus for good works, which God prepared beforehand that we should walk in them" (Ephesians 2:8–10).

Did you catch it? The Bible calls the plan of salvation a *creative act* of God! "We are His workmanship, created in Christ Jesus for good works." The Bible also says, "Therefore, if anyone is in Christ, he is a new creation; old things have passed away; behold, all things have become new" (2 Corinthians 5:17).

It's quite simple, really. The Sabbath was originally established at Creation as a day of rest and a memorial to God's creative power. After human beings sinned, it took on the added significance of being a celebration of God's power to save us and liberate us from the slavery of sin and re-create us in the image of Christ. The Sabbath has nothing to do with *earning* salvation. On the contrary, it marks the fact that we are *resting* in the knowledge that God has saved us and will bring us home.

This meaning in the Sabbath was so well understood by the early Christian church that the New Testament actually compares keeping the Sabbath to salvation by faith. In the book of Hebrews, the author briefly recounts the tragic story of Israel's failure to trust in God (see Hebrews 3:7–4:11). A more detailed account of what happened is found in the book of Numbers, where Israel is camped right up against the border of the Promised Land. God has been true to His word, faithfully leading them across the desert to the inheritance He promised to Abraham. Now the moment has come for them to take the final step of faith. They have plenty of reasons—from the parting of the Red Sea to the miraculous provision of food in the desert—to suspect that God will honor their faith and give them the land He has promised. Yet they flounder and fail. They decide to establish a committee to do a feasibility study of God's promise. They send twelve spies into Canaan to check things out: "And they returned from spying out the land after forty days. Now they departed and came back to Moses and Aaron and all the congregation of the children of Israel in the Wilderness of Paran, at Kadesh; they brought back word to them and to all the congregation, and showed them the fruit of the land. Then they told him, and said: 'We went to the land where you sent us. It truly flows with milk and honey, and this is its fruit' " (Numbers 13:25–27).

So far, so good! The spies come back with a report that the Promised Land is every bit as good as God had said it was. Then, as the Israelites are beginning to build a little courage, they suddenly shift gears. The spies continue their report: " 'Nevertheless the people who dwell in the land are strong; the cities are fortified and very large; moreover we saw the descendants of Anak there. The Amalekites dwell in the land of the South; the Hittites, the Jebusites, and the Amorites dwell in the mountains;

and the Canaanites dwell by the sea and along the banks of the Jordan' " (verses 28, 29).

Nevertheless. No word in the English language has been more devastating to the kingdom of heaven. With a single word, ten of the spies punctured the hopes of Israel by causing them to doubt God's promise. "It looks good, but there's no hope that we can take it. The people who live there are simply too much for us."

By all outward appearances, the unfaithful spies were right. Israel was a group of uneducated slaves who were untrained in the art of war. By anybody's estimation, they didn't stand a chance. When it comes to the problem of sin, we also don't stand a chance. Faced with our sins, we have to weep bitterly with the apostle Paul as he lamented his own slavery to sin: "O wretched man that I am! Who will deliver me from this body of death?" (Romans 7:24). We don't stand a chance. The devil is too big for us. Our sins look monstrous in the light of God's presence. There is no solution—except the promise of God.

Caleb, one of the twelve spies, understood this. " 'Let us go up at once and take possession,' " he said, " 'for we are well able to overcome it' " (Numbers 13:30). What was Caleb's secret? *He knew that victory was not contingent on Israel's ability, but upon God's power.* The conquest of Canaan was a matter of faith. Unfortunately, only two people believed in God's promise that day—Joshua and Caleb. The rest of Israel died in the wilderness. The book of Hebrews explains why: "For who, having heard, rebelled? Indeed, was it not all who came out of Egypt, led by Moses? Now with whom was He angry forty years? Was it not with those who sinned, whose corpses fell in the wilderness? And to whom did He swear that they would not enter His rest, but to those who did not obey? So we see that they could not enter in because of unbelief" (Hebrews 3:16–19).

Israel, whose journey across the desert symbolizes our journey into heaven's Promised Land, failed because of a lack of faith. It had nothing to do with the size of their army or their worthiness as genetic heirs of Abraham. It was all dependent on the promise of God and their willingness to believe it. If they had only stepped across the border, they would have discovered that God was indeed big enough to deal with any obstacle to salvation.

Here's the interesting part: in the same passage in Hebrews that deals with Israel's lack of faith and their inability to rest in God's promise, the author brings up the issue of our salvation—and he ties it to keeping the Sabbath! This is perhaps one of the most misunderstood passages in the Bible, so read it very carefully.

> Therefore, since a promise remains of entering His rest, let us fear lest any of you seem to have come short of it. For indeed the gospel was preached to us as well as to them; but the word which they heard did not profit them, not being mixed with faith in those who heard it.
>
> For we who have believed do enter that rest, as He has said:
>
> "So I swore in My wrath,
> They shall not enter My rest,"
>
> although the works were finished from the foundation of the world.
>
> For He has spoken in a certain place of the seventh day in this way: "And God rested on the seventh day from all His works"; and again in this place: "They shall not enter My rest" (Hebrews 4:1–5).

Notice how the author is making the same point we discussed earlier: the Sabbath is a symbol of *faith,* not works. Our salvation is not the result of our ability or works; it is the result of responding to the gospel message in *faith.* When we believe, we enter God's rest. Without faith, we cannot enter God's rest. Let's continue: "For if Joshua [Jesus] had given them rest, then He would not afterward have spoken of another day. There remains therefore a rest for the people of God. For he who has entered His rest has himself also ceased from his works as God did from His" (Hebrews 4:8–10).

Far from being an attempt trying to earn salvation through works, the Sabbath celebrates the fact that we are trusting in God alone for our salvation. Not only do we get to rest from six days of actual physical labor, we have a weekly reminder that we can rest in God's ability to save us from sin and ultimately deliver us to the Promised Land. It's the same meaning God added to the Sabbath after the Exodus—it is a celebration of both creation and re-creation. It's a clear sign that God understands the humiliation of our slavery to sin and that He's doing something about it.

"Who will deliver me from this body of death?" Paul asked. In the next verse, he gives the answer: "I thank God—through Jesus Christ our Lord!" (Romans 7:25).

The Sabbath, rightly understood, is not legalism at all. It's a matter of sheer faith. More than that, it's a legitimate way for suffering human beings to air their grievances against suffering; a way for us to shake a fist in the face of evil.

How?

We'll get to that. Before we do, we first need to unpack some hefty issues.

Chapter Three

Watch for Falling Angels

After Hurricane Katrina lashed out at the Gulf Coast, the pictures on CNN were like something out of a post-apocalyptic movie. Desperate homeowners were huddled on rooftops, waiting for a rescue helicopter. Thousands of homeless people holed up in the Superdome, where moments of anarchy broke out as people fought over things that would have never sparked a fight just one week earlier. We couldn't help wondering how a disaster of such appalling magnitude could possibly take place in our day and age. I remember thinking, *This doesn't happen here!*

The same was true when I witnessed the horrific events of 9/11. I was running late for work that morning, and I had the TV turned up in the bedroom so I could hear the morning traffic reports while I shaved in the bathroom. The traffic report never came. Instead, a voice broke into the usual newscast, announcing that there'd been an accident in New York City; an aircraft had collided with the World Trade Center. Curious, I walked into the bedroom. Sure enough, there was a smoldering black hole in the side of the tower. I watched for a few minutes as the newscasters speculated about what sort of aircraft had caused the damage and why it might be flying around downtown. And that's when I saw it—the second plane approaching. *This was no accident.*

Like everyone else that day, I forgot what I was supposed to be doing and sat down to watch for the rest of the morning. My wife was on the other side of the country, so I called her to get up and turn on the TV. "I'm not sure," I said, "but I think we might be at war." And the thought crossed my mind that morning, too, *This doesn't happen here!*

Don't get me wrong. It's not that North Americans should somehow be immune to large-scale catastrophes; it's just that we haven't really had that many. We're accustomed to seeing tragedies happen in other countries. We're left speechless when it happens at home. In a region of the world where we've generally come to trust our technology, our medicine, and our educational system (in spite of occasional murmurings), we tend to find acts of war and apocalyptic natural disasters out of place. We almost refuse to believe that it's real. We want heads to roll. We look for someone—anyone—to blame.

There's a statement in the Bible that most people glance over far too quickly, failing to comprehend its significance: "And war broke out in heaven" (Revelation 12:7). Shouldn't that statement shock us? War in *heaven*? That's not supposed to happen! If the Bible said there was to be war in the Middle East, we would understand. If it described a tribal conflict in Africa or a clash between South American drug lords, it wouldn't seem out of place. But war in *heaven*? Heaven!

It just doesn't fit our usual way of thinking. Heaven is the home of sinless angels and God Himself. There isn't supposed to be any suffering in a place like that, so how in the world could *war* possibly break out in heaven?

Based on the goodness of God, philosophers have long objected to the existence of evil—not just in heaven, but *anywhere* in the universe. "If God is all-knowing [omniscient]," they argue, "all-good [benevolent], and all-powerful [omnipotent], suffering should be, theoretically, impossible." In philosophical circles, this is known as "the problem of evil."

Atheists and skeptics love to point this out. "If your God is real," they claim, "surely He wouldn't allow the monstrous atrocities we have to live with. How can a God of love allow a killer earthquake to destroy thousands of innocent Chinese people? How can He stand by idly while the bodies of tens of thousands of Burmese cyclone victims wash down the rivers and survivors find themselves starving to death?" (These are catastrophes currently in the news. By the time you are reading these words, there will doubtless be scores of new examples for skeptics to point to.)

In addition to the perpetual problem of general human suffering, some unbelievers direct our attention to the sickening atrocities committed by so-called Christians during the Dark Ages. If God is real, and He created the human race, isn't He ultimately responsible for the rack and the fires of the Inquisition, the mutual slaughter of Protestants and Catholics? And what about the Bible itself? Why is it so violent? "Just what kind of God are you worshiping?" they ask.

At first glance, they seem to be right. There really are some pretty disturbing stories to be found between the covers of your Bible—stories of murder, betrayal, incest, you name it. If the Bible is supposed to be God's Book, and the people in it are supposed to be God's people, how in the world does some of that stuff happen?

One of the key problems is that very few critics have actually read the *whole* Bible carefully or honestly. Although some Christians tend to ignore the difficult passages of the Bible, its critics tend to ignore the all-important context of the rest of the Book, choosing, instead, to zero in on difficult passages and present them to the world out of the context in which they were intended to be understood. As a preacher friend used to say, "A text out of context is nothing but a pretext."

Years ago, when I was in South America, I met a man who had traveled a considerable distance to observe the technology we were using to broadcast a live television program to thousands of locations around the globe. I don't know who sent him, but he was clearly the wrong man for the job. He wasn't an electrical engineer; he was a public speaker. Far from being technically proficient, he actually struggled to figure out how the thermostat in his hotel room worked. I'm serious! I'll never forget his "careful" assessment of our control room (an operation that, frankly, makes my own head swim). He stuck his head through the door one afternoon for about two seconds, glanced at the many rows of sophisticated equipment, nodded as if he understood it all, and then left. That was it! He didn't take a single picture or jot down a single note! He had traveled halfway around the world for a two-second glance. I could be wrong, but I suspect he was unable to duplicate the control room when he returned home.

If a satellite uplink control room is sophisticated, the message of the Bible is even more so. Please don't misunderstand: the Bible's basic message is plain enough for a child to grasp in mere moments. The finer nuances, however, will provide you with enough material for a lifetime of careful study. " 'For as the heavens are higher than the earth,' " God says, " 'So are My ways higher than your ways, / And My thoughts than your thoughts' " (Isaiah 55:9). You simply can't learn everything there is to know about God with a casual glance, and that's precisely where most critics' arguments fall apart. They are nothing more than a casual glance at a very sophisticated subject.

As a university student, I remember becoming suspicious that some of my professors were assigning me a grade without reading my whole term paper. There were hundreds of students in every class, and I came to realize that very few professors had enough time in a week to carefully digest the contents of four hundred thirty-page term papers. Without fail, when I got my paper back, there would be a few notes scribbled in the margins of the first couple of pages and a few more notes on the last couple of pages. The twenty-six pages in the middle, however, were pristine. No one had read them. After all of the effort I poured into my papers (all right, into *some* of my papers), I felt cheated. How could my grade be accurate if the professor never actually *read* it?

I suspect God must feel a little frustrated when critics assign the Bible a grade after only skimming through it carelessly. They don't actually *read* it with an honest heart, and they are attempting to ruin peoples' faith with uninformed opinions. When you read the *whole* Book, the details start to make a lot of sense.

The truth is that the Bible presents our universe exactly the way it is—warts and all. It doesn't hide the truth, even when the truth is painful. In startling contrast to the mythology surrounding the heroes of other ancient cultures, Bible figures are not larger than life. Sure, there are miracles, but God performs them while the people He uses remain embarrassingly human. Noah got drunk. Abraham lied about his wife to save his own skin. Moses murdered an Egyptian in a fit of rage. Elijah became discouraged and wanted to die. David slept with another man's wife and had her husband killed to cover his tracks. The heroes of the Bible aren't larger than life; they're remarkably like *us.*

If the Bible were merely a bit of religious propaganda meant to promote the religion of Israel (as some scholars suggest), it's some of the worst propaganda ever written. There is no attempt to hide embarrassing blemishes or invent stories to keep people from noticing that something is wrong. In fact, the opposite is true: the Bible puts the blemishes at center stage and encourages us to look more closely. Essentially, God says, "Go ahead and look. I've got nothing to hide."

That's not the sort of thing a guilty person does. Ask a thief what he's got behind his back, and he tries to change the subject. Ask God why our world is so painful, and He says, "Here. Let me show you."

War broke out in heaven. If 9/11 made us feel sick to our stomachs, imagine how the angels must have felt when war erupted in Paradise. It's not supposed to happen. So why *did* it happen? The Bible provides an astonishing amount of detail. One of heaven's angels became dissatisfied with his position and had to be removed: "And war broke out in heaven: Michael and his angels fought with the dragon; and the dragon and his angels fought, but they did not prevail, nor was a place found for them in heaven any longer. So the great dragon was cast out, that serpent of old, called the Devil and Satan, who deceives the whole world; he was cast to the earth, and his angels were cast out with him" (Revelation 12:7–9).

Why did God kick Satan out of heaven? Did God simply get bored with him and say, "That's it. I'm tired of you. Out you go!" Of course not. Search through the Bible carefully, and you'll discover what the issue was:

> Moreover the word of the LORD came to me, saying,
> "Son of man, take up a lamentation for the king of Tyre, and say to him, 'Thus says the Lord GOD:
>
> "You were the seal of perfection,
> Full of wisdom and perfect in beauty" ' " (Ezekiel 28:11, 12).

In the prophetic portions of the Bible, God often uses an earthly object or person to help us understand an important spiritual principle. (For example, you'll find the city of Babylon mentioned several times in the book of Revelation. Even though the literal city of Babylon no longer existed when John wrote that book, it's used to portray rebellion against God.) In a fascinating passage of Ezekiel's prophecy, God uses the king of Tyre as a symbol to show us why He had to remove Satan (previously known as Lucifer) from heaven:

> " ' "You were in Eden, the garden of God;
> Every precious stone was your covering:
> The sardius, topaz, and diamond,
> Beryl, onyx, and jasper,
> Sapphire, turquoise, and emerald with gold.
> The workmanship of your timbrels and pipes
> Was prepared for you on the day you were created.

" ' "You were the anointed cherub who covers;
I established you;
You were on the holy mountain of God;
You walked back and forth in the midst of fiery stones.
You were perfect in your ways from the day you were
      created,
Till iniquity was found in you" ' " (verses 13–15).

This passage brings a number of important issues to the foreground: (1) Lucifer was the "anointed cherub who covers," (2) he was once "perfect," and (3) "iniquity was found" in him. Let's examine these three points in turn, because they tell an important story.

1. Lucifer was the "cherub who covers." The ark of the covenant was one of the most important artifacts in the ancient world. It was located in the innermost chamber of the Old Testament sanctuary, a room known as the "Most Holy Place." According to the Bible, the very presence of God would take up residence between the two golden angels on top of the ark and communicate with His people (see, for example, Exodus 25:22). No one was allowed to enter the Most Holy Place (except the high priest, who was allowed access only once a year).

The book of Hebrews tells us that everything in the Old Testament sanctuary represented a greater reality in heaven (see Hebrews 8:1–5; 9:1–5). The ark was a symbol of God's throne in heaven, and the two angels affixed to the top of the ark were known as *covering* cherubs, because their wings covered the top of the ark (see Exodus 25:20; 37:9; Hebrews 9:5). Lucifer was once a "cherub who covers," and while we don't know a lot about his actual job description, it was apparently one of the most exalted positions in heaven, right next to God's throne. This means that Lucifer was once the highest of all angels, holding a position of great honor.

2. Lucifer was perfect when he was created. You wouldn't expect anything less of a creature designed by God. He simply doesn't do second-rate work. You'll notice in the Creation account (see

Genesis 1) that God steps back at the end of each day and says, "It is good!" At the end of the Creation week, God says, "It is *very* good!" We have no reason to believe that He did a lesser job of creating the angels.

3. Iniquity was found in Lucifer. It was not *created* in Lucifer. This is an important distinction. Many people assume that because God gave birth to the universe, He must have also created everything in it, including evil. But the Bible tells us quite plainly that God did not *create* a devil. He *discovered* a devil, and there's a world of difference. Hitler's mother didn't give birth to a genocidal maniac; she gave birth to an innocent baby boy. Like any new mother, she had dreams and aspirations for her son, and I highly doubt that she wanted him to become world famous as the author of the Holocaust. Likewise, God didn't give birth to a fallen angel. He discovered one.

How is it possible for a perfect angel to fall? Was there some sort of fatal design flaw in God's work? If the passage in Ezekiel were the only information we had, our picture would be incomplete, and we'd be left to speculate. Fortunately, the Bible gives us much more. Take a look at the fall of Lucifer as described by the prophet Isaiah:

> "How you are fallen from heaven,
> O Lucifer, son of the morning!
> How you are cut down to the ground,
> You who weakened the nations!
> For you have said in your heart:
> 'I will ascend into heaven,
> I will exalt my throne above the stars of God;
> I will also sit on the mount of the congregation
> On the farthest sides of the north;
> I will ascend above the heights of the clouds,
> I will be like the Most High' " (Isaiah 14:12–14).

Lucifer mentions the word *I* five times. "I will ascend into heaven." "I will be like the Most High." The problem with Lucifer was his sense of pride. Dissatisfied with his position as a covering cherub, he longed for something higher. He couldn't help but notice that, as high as his position was, it simply wasn't the highest one in heaven. God Himself held a much higher post, and it began to bother Lucifer that he wasn't actually at the top of heaven's pecking order. He wanted something more. He wanted *God's* place.

Of course, that raises another good question: why would God create angels that had the ability to turn against Him?

The answer is as simple as it is profound. The kingdom of God is founded on the principle of selfless love. John makes the simple assertion, "God is love" (1 John 4:16). Genuine love is not possible apart from the power to choose. If you don't have the ability to choose *not* to love someone, love becomes meaningless. If God didn't give His creatures the option of choosing against Him, their loyalty and friendship would be empty.

The Bible says that we were created in the image of God, so it's not hard for us to imagine why God would go through the trouble of creating a universe with the potential for rebellion. We can find the reason in our own relationships. When I offer my children a choice between a battery-operated puppy from Toys "R" Us and a real live dog, they always tell me they want the real thing. Why? Some of the mechanical puppies at the toy store are remarkable: they can bark, roll over, and respond to your commands. When you're tired of them, you can simply turn them off! Compared to the real thing, robotic dogs are much easier. Real puppies can make a terrible mess. They chew on your favorite socks, scratch up the furniture, and have horrific "accidents" on the living room carpet. They run away or bite the neighbor kids. Yet somehow, in spite of the risks, many people are drawn to real dogs. They figure the potential for disaster is a risk worth taking because the *relationship* can be so rewarding.

Ask yourself why human beings would consider having children.

The Sign

If you think about child rearing simply in terms of cost, few people would ever choose to have a baby. Not only do children cost hundreds of thousands of dollars to raise, but the potential for heartache is enormous. Your child might make very costly mistakes. He might actually turn his back on everything you believe in and have nothing to do with you. He might marry poorly or die foolishly. We have thousands of examples of this sort of pain living all around us, and yet most people long to have children anyway. The *relationship* seems worth the risk.

If God were simply looking for a labor force when He created the angels, I suppose robots would have done the trick. But God wants something more from His creatures; He wants a meaningful relationship. There would be no joy for God in knowing that the angels served Him only because it was hardwired into their circuit boards. Without a choice, there is no relationship.

I love coming home at the end of a long trip overseas. My two kids usually post a large homemade sign over the front hall that proclaims: "Welcome Home, Daddy!" in a dazzling array of crayon colors. As soon as they hear the screen door squeaking on its hinges, they drop whatever they're doing and run screaming through the house: *"Daddy's home!"* I've got to say, that's pretty cool. Why does it thrill me? I have a family that *wants* me to be there. My kids can't wait for me to get home. And my wife chooses to stay with me—if you can believe it—day after day. It brings me a lot of joy, because I know they *mean* it. They really love me. But if they were chained to the wall, held against their will, unable to leave, the whole relationship would suddenly become a joyless farce.

Unfortunately, we spend so much time theorizing about God that we forget a simple fact: God has *feelings*. The Bible reveals Him as a Person—happy, angry, saddened, worried, weeping, and even singing. He is not simply the cosmic control center for the universe; He longs to have meaningful relationships every bit as much as we do. In fact, the reason we crave meaningful relationships ourselves is because we were made in His image.

Why would He create a universe that has the ability to choose against Him? Why take such a colossal risk? It's really quite simple. If everyone can leave, but chooses to stay, the relationship is real. It's voluntary. If Lucifer didn't have the ability to rebel against God—if he were created *without* a choice—how valuable would his allegiance to God be? In order for the universe to function the way God intended, and in order for the universe to accurately reflect God's loving, selfless nature, there had to be freedom of choice. Anything else would fall incredibly short of God's magnificent character.

So what brought Lucifer down? His *pride.* At some point, Lucifer quit studying the selfless, loving character of God and began to focus on himself. He quit living for others and started serving self. His opinion of himself became greatly inflated, and even though he is the only angel in the Bible who actually gets honorable mention for his attractive appearance (see Ezekiel 28:12), his beauty quickly vanished in the ugly shadow of his pride. Just think about the egotistical people you've met over the years. Some of them were actually good-looking at first sight; but the moment they opened their mouths, the physical attraction vanished because there's nothing beautiful about haughty arrogance.

A friend of mine used to tell the story of a pretty girl at his university campus. He desperately wanted to meet her. One day he planted himself in the middle of the path she normally took to class so she would have to stop and he would have a chance to talk to her. When she eventually came down the path and was forced to stop, his mind went blank, and he searched frantically for something meaningful to say. His face turned red, and he clumsily blurted out, "You are the *prettiest* girl I've ever seen!"

"I know!" she declared haughtily.

"After that, she didn't seem beautiful to me anymore," he told me.

Why? Pride is ugly.

Exercising his right to choose *against* God, Lucifer lost his

God-given beauty and became a raging egomaniac. He fancied himself to be more important than he really was, and he began to spread his personal dissatisfaction around the courts of heaven. He whispered his doubts about God's character into the ears of other angels. We obviously don't have a transcript of what he said, but it's not hard to imagine:

- "God doesn't let me in on the really big decisions. You've got to wonder what He doesn't want us to see."
- "Maybe God doesn't really know what He's doing, and He's afraid we'll notice that He's not really in control."
- "Maybe this whole system is a little unfair, and look at all those moral rules God has! I mean, did He ever put it to a vote?"

When it became obvious that Lucifer was set in his ways, the covering cherub simply had to be removed. A third of heaven's angels went with him.[1] It was a terrible loss to God's kingdom. The Bible reveals that the number of angels that stayed behind—the remaining two-thirds—still was in the range of hundreds of millions (see Daniel 7:10; Revelation 5:11). That means a *lot* of angels left!

So why didn't God simply eliminate Lucifer?

That's a good question. If God is truly all-powerful, surely He was capable of wiping out the devil before the problem spread across the universe. Why didn't He do it? The answer is elegantly simple. Given the high number of angels that rebelled, we can presume that Lucifer's rumors about God had spread throughout the ranks of heaven. What impression would be created among the angels if God suddenly snuffed him out? Put it in human terms, and it's easy to understand. What would happen if one of my brothers had been whispering uncertainties about my father's character for a number of weeks and one day, when I came home from school, he was suddenly missing?

---

1. See Revelation 12:4. In the prophetic passages of the Bible, *stars* are often used to represent angels. See Job 38:7; Revelation 1:20.

"Hey, Mom," I ask, "where's Kevin? Hasn't he come home yet?"

"Your father took him out back last night and shot him. I think he's buried somewhere in the backyard. Why do you ask?"

From that moment on, you can be sure that I would be a perfectly obedient child—for as long as it would take to grow up and move out! My relationship would be based on *fear* rather than love and trust. It wouldn't be a real relationship at all. If God had simply terminated Lucifer the moment the trouble started, imagine the impact it would have on the other angels. What would they think? *Maybe Lucifer was right! Obviously, God has something to hide. Why else would He just kill him like that?*

The problem was enormous: How does God preserve what's left without taking away the freedom to choose? How can He eliminate rebellion permanently without changing the voluntary nature of His relationship to His creatures? Wisely, God has chosen to allow Lucifer to play out his rebellion in front of the entire universe so that, in the end, we can all see for ourselves what a world without God looks like. Sometimes, the only way to learn that you shouldn't touch a hot stove is to touch one—once. When we've lived in this sin-plagued place for a while—and then suddenly we find ourselves restored to Paradise—no one is going to choose rebellion again. We will have seen firsthand how much pain it causes to be separated from God. It's the ideal solution: God preserves our liberty, and at the same time, He eliminates all future temptation to rebel. Forever.

But why should humans suffer? It's simple. We could have said *No* to the serpent in Eden. We had a choice. If we had stayed loyal to God, the issue would have come to crisis right then and there. But instead, we chose rebellion. In a moment of weakness, we doubted God's word and allowed ourselves to wander over to the other side of the fence. Since that moment, God has been trying to woo us back.

Chapter Four

What Lucifer Really Wants

I used to be under the impression that what Lucifer really wants is for people to do bad things. I thought his job was to hang out on your left shoulder dressed in a red jumpsuit and whisper naughty suggestions in your ear. He was ugly—horns, hooves, a tail—you get the picture. But according to the Bible, the devil isn't ugly (see Ezekiel 28:11, 12), and his goal is not simply to get you to do something wrong. The issues are much bigger.

If human beings—created in the image of God—routinely violate God's moral principles, it discredits the idea that His requirements are reasonable or that obeying them is even *possible*. It casts a shadow of doubt over the viability of God's government. "See?" the devil exults as we find ourselves irresistibly attracted to sin and helplessly enslaved to it, "I *told* you there was something wrong with God's way! *No one* can live up to His expectations!"

It's not just about bad deeds. Lucifer wants more than that. He wants to sit on God's throne.

"For you have said in your heart:
'I will ascend into heaven,
I will exalt my throne above the stars of God;
I will also sit on the mount of the congregation
On the farthest sides of the north;
I will ascend above the heights of the clouds,
I will be like the Most High' " (Isaiah 14:13, 14).

Lucifer wants to be *worshiped*. He craves the adoration that rightfully belongs only to God. The devil has forgotten the very first principle of the kingdom of heaven—selfless love. If he *did* sit on the throne of the universe, it would be for all the wrong reasons. He doesn't want to rule because it would bring the greatest happiness to the universe; he wants to rule because he's obsessed with himself.

Only God is qualified to sit on the throne, because only God can *create*.

Whenever the living creatures give glory and honor and thanks to Him who sits on the throne, who lives forever and ever, the twenty-four elders fall down before Him who sits on the throne and worship Him who lives forever and ever, and cast their crowns before the throne, saying:

"You are worthy, O Lord,
To receive glory and honor and power;
For You created all things,
And by Your will they exist and were created" (Revelation 4:9–11).

God occupies the throne because He alone holds the keys to life. No one else is capable of producing life. Human scientists, for example, can *clone* life, but they can't *create* it. Medical technology can revive an *almost dead* person, but not someone who's been dead for four days—a feat that Jesus pulled off at the grave of Lazarus. Only God holds the keys of life, and for that reason, only God is capable of knowing what's best for living creatures. He's the only One who could possibly make us happy or make us feel fulfilled. We worship God—we focus our entire existence on Him—because we were made by Him. The Bible repeats this fact many times:

The Sign

Then Hezekiah prayed before the LORD, and said: "O LORD God of Israel, the One who dwells between the cherubim, You are God, You alone, of all the kingdoms of the earth. You have made heaven and earth" (2 Kings 19:15).

"You alone are the LORD;
You have made heaven,
The heaven of heavens, with all their host,
The earth and all things on it,
The seas and all that is in them,
And You preserve them all.
The host of heaven worships You" (Nehemiah 9:6).

Our help is in the name of the LORD,
Who made heaven and earth (Psalm 124:8).

Thus you shall say to them: "The gods that have not made the heavens and the earth shall perish from the earth and from under these heavens."

He has made the earth by His power,
He has established the world by His wisdom,
And has stretched out the heavens at His discretion (Jeremiah 10:11, 12).

And he said to them, "I am a Hebrew; and I fear the LORD, the God of heaven, who made the sea and the dry land" (Jonah 1:9).

So when they heard that, they raised their voice to God with one accord and said: "Lord, You are God, who made heaven and earth and the sea, and all that is in them" (Acts 4:24).

But when the apostles Barnabas and Paul heard this, they tore their clothes and ran in among the multitude, crying out and saying, "Men, why are you doing these things? We also are men with the same nature as you, and preach to you that you should turn from these vain things to the living God, who made the heaven, the earth, the sea, and all things that are in them" (Acts 14:14, 15).

Then I saw another angel flying in the midst of heaven, having the everlasting gospel to preach to those who dwell on the earth—to every nation, tribe, tongue, and people— saying with a loud voice, "Fear God and give glory to Him, for the hour of His judgment has come; and worship Him who made heaven and earth, the sea and springs of water" (Revelation 14:6, 7).

Lucifer simply doesn't qualify for worship, because it is not within his power to create anything. In fact, throughout thousands of years of human misery, he has clearly demonstrated that he is utterly incapable of making anybody truly happy. Those who submit to his will find themselves broken and miserable. He " 'was a murderer from the beginning, and does not stand in the truth, because there is no truth in him' " (John 8:44). Our broken world stands as a powerful testimony to this fact.

Blinded by pride and ambition, however, the devil refuses to believe that he has lost. He is still determined to occupy God's place. And if he can't literally push God off the throne of the universe, perhaps he can remove Him from the throne of human hearts. Maybe he can persuade us to think of God as something other than a Creator.

Enter the theory of evolution. For millennia, it seemed perfectly obvious to us that Someone created our world. The planet is so finely balanced, so finely tuned to support life, that it seemed self-evident that Someone designed it. Then suddenly, about a hundred and fifty years ago, a new[1] theory was placed on the table—the idea that life somehow came into being all by itself.

Scientifically speaking, we know this is an impossible proposition. Life does not spontaneously come from nonliving material. The elements simply cannot come to life all on their own. This has been well established since Louis Pasteur proved it beyond all shadow of doubt—in the same century that Darwin wrote *The Origin of Species.* Of course, the only logical alternative to the spontaneous generation of life is the existence of a Creator. Herein lies the real issue at stake in the creation/evolution debate. Geneticist Richard Lewontin makes a remarkable admission:

> We take the side of science in spite of the patent absurdity of some of its constructs, in spite of its failure to fulfill many of its extravagant promises of health and life, in spite of the tolerance of the scientific community of unsubstantiated just-so stories, because we have a prior commitment, a commitment to materialism. It is not that the methods and institutions of science somehow compel us to accept a material explanation of the phenomenal world, but on the contrary, that we are forced by our a priori adherence to material causes to create an apparatus of investigation and a set of concepts that produce material explanations, no matter how counter-intuitive, no matter how mystifying to the uninitiated. Moreover, that materialism is an absolute, for we cannot allow a Divine Foot in the door.[2]

What is Mr. Lewontin saying? He admits that the basic premise of evolutionary science is absurd, but that to accept anything other than a strictly material explanation for our world would be to admit to the existence of God. Rather than do that,

---

1. The theory of evolution wasn't actually new; it predates Charles Darwin. He simply gave it its current incarnation.

2. Nicholas Comninellis, *Darwin's Demise,* ed. Joe White (Green Forest, Ark.: Master Books, 2001), 137.

we deliberately accept what is impossible—the notion that life came about by accident. And to make that seem more feasible, we have stretched out the history of our planet by *billions* of years, suggesting that anything might be possible given enough time.

Think about this carefully. This isn't really a matter of science versus faith; every year, new evidence suggests that the theory of evolution is fundamentally flawed. It's more a matter of who gets to sit on the throne of our hearts. It's a matter of where our loyalties lie.

In what some people consider to be the oldest book in the Bible, God pulls back the curtains of the cosmos and gives us a peek at what's happening behind the scenes. Before we look at it, however, let's set the stage. Our first parents fell into sin because Lucifer convinced them to question God's word. "Now the serpent was more cunning than any beast of the field which the LORD God had made. And he said to the woman, 'Has God indeed said, "You shall not eat of every tree of the garden"?' " (Genesis 3:1).

The devil's methods have changed very little in thousands of years. He doesn't challenge God's word outright; instead, he simply raises doubts. *Did God really say that?* When Adam and Eve chose to believe the serpent, they questioned God's word, which means they also questioned His trustworthiness. When God arrived that evening to speak to Adam, human rebellion had already become so entrenched that he tried to blame God for what happened! " 'The woman whom *You* gave to be with me, she gave me of the tree, and I ate' " (Genesis 3:12, emphasis supplied). In a single act of disobedience, we chimed in with newfound doubts about God's ability to govern, and we yielded our dominion over the planet to Lucifer.

In the book of Job, God pulls back the curtain to show us what's really going on. After introducing the main character—a man who was "blameless and upright"—the story begins with the devil showing up at a conference in heaven: "Now there was a day when the sons of God came to present themselves before the

Lord, and Satan also came among them. And the Lord said to Satan, 'From where do you come?' So Satan answered the Lord and said, 'From going to and fro on the earth, and from walking back and forth on it' " (Job 1:6, 7).

In biblical times, placing your feet on something was a way of claiming it as your own. When God promised Abraham the land of Canaan, He said, " 'Arise, walk in the land through its length and its width, for I give it to you' " (Genesis 13:17). When Israel was about to inherit the Promised Land, God said to Joshua, " 'Every place that the sole of your foot will tread upon I have given you' " (Joshua 1:3). When ancient soldiers placed their foot on the neck of a slain enemy, it was a way of saying, "I own you." Satan is making a bold statement in front of the universe—his kingdom is growing. Not only has a third of the angels followed him in rebellion, the citizens of planet Earth have also joined him now. He's been "walking back and forth" on the earth because he now *owns* it.

But again, human rebellion isn't the devil's real objective. Nor is ownership of the planet. He craves *worship*. Many years later, as he attempted to derail the ministry of Christ, he offered to give our planet back if Jesus would only bow down and worship at his feet. "Again, the devil took Him up on an exceedingly high mountain, and showed Him all the kingdoms of the world and their glory. And he said to Him, 'All these things I will give You if You will fall down and worship me' " (Matthew 4:8, 9).

Lucifer has a one-track mind. He wants just one thing: the throne of the universe. In the book of Job, he parades his trophy— our planet—in front of the heavenly council, trying to prove a point. His empire is growing. That's when God interjects; "Then the Lord said to Satan, 'Have you considered My servant Job, that there is none like him on the earth, a blameless and upright man, one who fears God and shuns evil?' " (Job 1:8).

Essentially, God says, "Not so fast, Satan. You don't own the *whole* planet. There's a man down there whose heart, in spite of your claims, still belongs to Me." Even though the human race was clearly in a state of rebellion, not all was lost. The devil had deliberately chosen to rebel against God, but the human race was *deceived*. There was still hope for us, and ever since the Fall, there have always been those whose hearts still belong to God.

Not willing to admit that he was wrong in front of the heavenly council, the devil began to question Job's motives. "Of *course* Job follows You," he said. "Just look at his situation. He's a rich man! Obviously, he's following You for the benefits of membership. If You just stopped giving him stuff—if You cut off the perks—he'd curse You in a heartbeat" (see Job 1:9–11).

The devil's claim was that, given a real choice, no one would willingly put himself under God's government. Job was clearly faking it. If the material benefits of membership in God's kingdom were suddenly gone, he'd quickly switch sides. "All right," God replied, "here's the deal. You can take away his stuff, but you may not lay a finger on him" (see verse 12).

Why does God allow it? Remember the circumstances: a sizable part of God's creation is in rebellion, claiming that God's government is untenable. In order to bring the conflict to a satisfactory close without violating freedom of choice, God is allowing the devil to show himself for what he really is in front of the entire universe. Satan has now suggested that human beings are just as selfish as he is. They have no interest in a genuine relationship with the Creator; in fact, they follow God only in order to reap some sort of benefit.

As the story unfolds, the devil does his utmost to shake Job's faith. When bankruptcy wasn't enough to make him turn against the Creator, the devil ruined his health. Tragically, that was enough to make Job's wife turn against God (see Job 2:9), but Job stood firm. Ultimately—even though Job, like us, had trouble understanding *why* these sorts of things happen—nothing could make him turn against God.

Why do human beings suffer? The story of Job makes several important points:

- We have yielded control of the planet to someone who is incapable of governing it, and we are reaping the rewards of that decision.
- The devil is interested in turning our hearts against the Creator, so he creates opportunities for human suffering and then tries to pin the blame on God.
- If God were to intervene every time humans suffered, we would fail to reap the consequences of our freewill decision to surrender our allegiance to fallen angels, and nothing would be learned.
- Additionally, Satan could cry foul by pointing out to the universe that God is interfering in his government and not *really* giving people the opportunity to choose an alternative to Him.

Of course, the issues are more complex than these short summary statements. But the central point of Job is clear: God has people on this planet who, in spite of what their senses might tell them for the moment, choose to believe Him. Fallen angels hate these people; in fact, they'll do whatever it takes to disrupt their relationship with the Creator. They know that anyone who stays true to God and develops a personal relationship with Him is going to discover that Satan has been lying. They do their utmost to convince us that God is arbitrary and severe, and they expend unbelievable amounts of energy trying to cover up the truth about the Creator: "But even if our gospel is veiled, it is veiled to those who are perishing, whose minds the god of this age has blinded, who do not believe, lest the light of the gospel of the glory of Christ, who is the image of God, should shine on them" (2 Corinthians 4:3, 4).

So what does all this have to do with the Sabbath? More than you might think.

Chapter Five

Choosing Sides

You see them in the mall—sullen teenagers walking fifteen feet behind their parents, hoping desperately that no one will think they're related. At the moment, fortunately, my girls are young, and they still think their daddy is about the smartest man in the world. I have been assured by many fathers, however, that the situation will change, and I will soon be demoted to the position of dumbest man on earth.

In fact, I've already had a taste of what's coming. When my daughter was in the second grade, my wife and I were in the habit of walking her to the classroom door when we dropped her off for school. One morning, as I pulled up to the school, Natalie suddenly asked, "Daddy, do you think you could drop me off at the *corner*?"

Ouch! I knew that she loved me and that the kids had probably been teasing her about being a baby, but still, I couldn't help but feel the sting of her desire to distance herself from my company.

Every father wants to be loved by his children, and God the Father is no exception. As the human race fell into sin, a tragic thing happened. We deliberately distanced ourselves from God. We drove a wedge into the relationship. With earthly fathers, the process is natural. If all goes well, our children are *supposed* to grow up and leave us. But with God, it was never supposed to happen. We were already grown up and in a healthy relationship with our heavenly Father. Yet we chose to distance ourselves, and since that moment, the human race has fallen into two distinct camps—those (like Job) whose humble allegiance belongs to God and those whose proud loyalty belongs to fallen angels.

Since our fall into sin, the story of planet Earth has been portrayed in the Bible as a tale of two cities. On the one hand, you have the city of Babylon, which represents human self-sufficiency. Established on the plains of Shinar after the destruction of the Tower of Babel, it is an outgrowth of human pride. King Nebuchadnezzar eloquently summarized the attitude of Babylon: " 'Is not this great Babylon, that I have built for a royal dwelling by my mighty power and for the honor of my majesty?' " (Daniel 4:30). Nothing could have been further from the truth. The prophet Daniel had already informed the king that " 'the God of heaven has given you a kingdom, power, strength, and glory' " (Daniel 2:37). In the book of Revelation, the city of Babylon is used as a symbol of spiritual confusion, pride, and self-sufficiency.

On the other hand, there is the city of Jerusalem, which was the capital city of God's people. The temple was located there, and during Solomon's reign, the actual presence of God filled the sanctuary (see 1 Kings 8:10, 11). There was nothing self-sufficient about Jerusalem because it was the focal point for a sacrificial system that pointed the Israelites to utter dependence on Christ for salvation. In the book of Revelation, Jerusalem is used as a symbol of the permanent home of those whose hearts belong to the Creator.

The book of Revelation, itself, is like a lens, focusing the content of the entire Bible—the story of salvation—into a few short chapters. It cuts right to the chase and identifies the most important issues. In the center of the book (where ancient authors usually placed their main point) God gets to the heart of the matter. There we see the conflict between God and Lucifer erupt, and we see the devil's determination to eliminate those whose hearts remain true to God (see chapter 12). In chapter 13, the focus is on the devil's side of the conflict, revealing his ultimate plan to force the world to worship him. In chapter 14, we see the other side of the conflict—God's faithful people, their message to the world, and the ultimate destiny of those on both sides of the battle.

There is something fascinating in the opening verses of chapter 14. John writes, "Then I looked, and behold, a Lamb standing on Mount Zion, and with Him one hundred and forty-four thousand, having His Father's name written on their foreheads" (Revelation 14:1).

God's faithful people have His name written on their foreheads! The *forehead* represents the place where we make our decisions. Today, we know that the frontal lobe of the brain is located right behind our forehead, which is the part of the brain we use to make moral judgments. It's where we weigh the future and make decisions about it. It's also where we make choices between right and wrong, between good and bad consequences. God's faithful people have His name written there. In spite of Lucifer's best attempts to persuade them against their Creator, they have made a solid decision—like Job did—to stand with Him. They have come to the irreversible conclusion that God is everything He's ever claimed to be: merciful, just, and loving. They "follow the Lamb wherever He goes" (verse 4).

What's in a name? In the biblical world, parents didn't give their children names because they liked the sound of them. Names were chosen carefully, because mothers and fathers hoped the character traits represented by the name would become the character traits of their children. Your name was more than just a label; it was a synopsis of your character. Even though we are decidedly less careful about naming people in the twenty-first century, this way of thinking has not been entirely lost. We still complain about people "ruining our good name" when they make insinuations about our character.

One of the reasons Jesus took on human form and lived among us was to rip the mask off Lucifer's lies and reveal the truth about God's character. Notice what Jesus said at the end of His ministry about His completed mission:

"I have manifested Your name to the men whom You have given Me out of the world. They were Yours, You gave them to Me, and they have kept Your word. Now they have known that all things which You have given Me are from You. For I have given to them the words which You have given Me; and they have received them, and have known surely that I came forth from You; and they have believed that You sent Me" (John 17:6–8).

"And I have declared to them Your name, and will declare it, that the love with which You loved Me may be in them, and I in them" (John 17:26).

God's name is more than simply a label we apply to the Supreme Being. It is a picture of His character, which is why you find many names for God used throughout the Bible. Each of them represents an important character trait and reveals something essential about God's nature. When Jesus said that He showed the disciples His Father's name, it's another way of saying He faithfully represented God's character to the world. And when the Bible says that God's faithful people have His name written in their foreheads, it means that after examining the evidence, they've made an intelligent decision about God's character and that their allegiance belongs to Him. You see their decision in the song of Moses and the Lamb.

They sing the song of Moses, the servant of God, and the song of the Lamb, saying:

"Great and marvelous are Your works,
Lord God Almighty!
Just and true are Your ways,
O King of the saints!

Who shall not fear You, O Lord, and glorify Your
 name?
For You alone are holy.
For all nations shall come and worship before You,
For Your judgments have been manifested" (Revela-
tion 15:3, 4).

These people are utterly convinced that God is everything
He's ever claimed to be. That His decisions have always been
right. In spite of the devil's best efforts to besmirch God's character, they can see that He is just and true. In spite of Lucifer's attempts to garner their support in his bid for the throne, they have
decided that God *alone* is holy.

It is precisely on this front that the devil launches his boldest
attacks. The thought that God still has faithful followers infuri-
ates him, because he knows that those who continue to follow
their Creator will ultimately expose him as a murderer and a liar.
Bible prophecy provides the chilling details of Lucifer's master
plan: "Let no one deceive you by any means; for that Day will not
come unless the falling away comes first, and the man of sin is
revealed, the son of perdition, who opposes and exalts himself
above all that is called God or that is worshiped, so that he sits as
God in the temple of God, showing himself that he is God"
(2 Thessalonians 2:3, 4).

Here, Paul clearly identifies two things that will happen before Jesus returns: (1) a "falling away," and (2) the appearance of
the "man of sin." Then he adds a detail that we shouldn't miss:
"For the mystery of lawlessness is already at work" (verse 7).

Something was already at work back in Paul's day that would
ultimately set the stage for a global deception. He calls it the "mystery of lawlessness." (In some translations of the Bible, it's described as the "mystery of iniquity." *Iniquity* is a word that simply
means "lawlessness." When the Bible says that "iniquity" was
found in Lucifer, it sheds a great deal of light on the nature of his

rebellion. He became lawless, challenging the very laws of God's government.)

Today, we can see that Paul was absolutely right. In our day and age, lawlessness has grown to epic proportions. Even though we in the West like to think of ourselves as a Christian society, we continue to have some of the highest crime rates on the planet. In fact, an Internet list of the most dangerous nations on earth gives the United States of America honorable mention. Of course, the Internet is not always a reliable source of information, but the listing had an uncomfortable ring of truth about it.

> For the average traveller, the USA is fairly safe, but the numbers do not lie. There are more than 200 million guns in the USA and more than 50 murders a day, 10 times the rate of Germany. Nearly 5000 people die a year in truck crashes, about 6000 pedestrians die on the streets and 31000 people end their own lives. The USA now leads all nations in violent crime and leads all nations with incarcerations now standing at 2.3 million. American citizens also make up the greatest number of criminals serving time in overseas prisons. Militias, hate groups, and other right wing radicals all spread their message of violence and are known to throw around the odd pipe-bomb.[1]

Today, many people insist that Western civilization is based on the moral laws of the Judeo-Christian tradition. Yet if that's true, why do we live with so many locks and deadbolts? Not too long ago, we felt much more secure than we do now. My mother used to send us children outside to play after breakfast, and we were essentially allowed to go wherever we wanted. The only rule was that we had to come home when the siren on the fire station (which sounded at noon) signaled that it was lunchtime. When

---

1. Jamie Frater, "Top 10 Most Dangerous Places on Earth," List Universe, http://listverse.com/travel/top-10-most-dangerous-places-on-earth.

Mom ran into the grocery store, she left the car running, and my brothers and I waited for her outside.

One generation later, the world is a much different place. My wife and I wouldn't dream of giving our children free rein in the streets, and when I'm not home, my wife almost always keeps the front door locked. We never leave the keys in the car, and like millions of other people, we're immediately suspicious of the motives of anybody who knocks on our door. Our moral situation here in the West has become so bad that I've heard people of other faiths make fun of us overseas. They see the immoral themes of Hollywood, and they hear the suggestive lyrics of our music, and they laugh. *What kind of religion produces that sort of filth?* they wonder.

In light of the great conflict portrayed in the Bible, can you see what's happening? God's name is being tarnished by the very people who claim to follow Him. It's all part of a master plan to discredit the Creator. In another prophetic passage, Paul reveals to what extent the devil will be successful: "But know this, that in the last days perilous times will come: For men will be lovers of themselves, lovers of money, boasters, proud, blasphemers, disobedient to parents, unthankful, unholy, unloving, unforgiving, slanderers, without self-control, brutal, despisers of good, traitors, headstrong, haughty, lovers of pleasure rather than lovers of God, having a form of godliness but denying its power" (2 Timothy 3:1–5).

Take another moment and read that passage again. It's alarming just how accurate it is. Today, in the wake of the sexual revolution, the wreckage of our families lies strewn in the streets. Our prisons are overcrowded. The courthouses are full of lawsuits. Convinced that our existence is merely an accident of the universe instead of a deliberate act of God, we have made pleasure-seeking our number one priority. We've actually become so steeped in lawless living that it's hard for us to remember that it hasn't always been this way.

What happened?

One of the key factors that has led to our moral decline is a relatively new idea known as situation ethics, developed in the 1960s by American professor Joseph Fletcher. His theory taught that no action is inherently wrong if you can find a good reason for doing it. Any act can be considered ethical depending on the circumstances that led to it. The end result of this idea has been a generation that quit believing in absolute standards of right and wrong.

You can easily witness the fruits of this kind of thinking on such daytime TV talk shows as *Maury Povich* or worse yet, *Jerry Springer*. The quality of most of these programs has slid so far downhill, it's embarrassing. Most episodes are a display of human misery, in which people with aberrant lifestyles or who are guilty of incredible moral indiscretions are paraded across the stage. Topics include such uplifting themes as "I'm a Prostitute," "Our Baby May Not Be Yours," and "My Controlling Husband Makes Me Sell My Body." Ostensibly, the purpose of these programs is to "educate" the audience on important moral issues, but the truth is that we've come to like being entertained with increasingly shocking sins.

Where does situation ethics fit into this scenario?

When the audience boos or hisses at the perpetrator of a distasteful moral indiscretion—for example, a man who has been cheating on his wife with her sister—the guilty party will usually respond by saying some form of this argument: "You can't judge me, because you don't know me!" That's the fruit of situation ethics. According to this concept, there is no absolute right or wrong—there is only what is right or wrong for you. You can't label something as morally wrong, because there is no such thing. You can only indicate that you find it distasteful.

This system of belief was being taught in philosophy classes when I went to school. The professor used to ask us questions such as, "Is it wrong to torture a child?" We assured him that torturing children is absolutely wrong, at which point he asked the question again, but with a slightly different twist: "Is it *always* wrong to torture a child? What if you've been in a car accident? Your family is pinned inside the vehicle and will die without medical attention. You knock on the door of a nearby house, asking to use the phone, but the lady of the house is afraid of you and refuses to let you in. That's when you spot her little boy playing in the yard. Would it be wrong to twist that boy's arm in order to convince the lady to open the door? You'd be saving lives!"

Pay careful attention to what's happening in this argument. The professor is using an unlikely scenario to confuse the issue. More than one generation has now come through school learning that there is no such thing as black and white when it comes to moral issues—only gray. We've been told that no one can sit in judgment on the actions of another, and we're paying a considerable price for this kind of thinking. A few years ago, a surprising article in *U.S. News & World Report* unmasked the moral confusion our young people live with. According to this article, one college professor reported that "10 percent to 20 percent of his students could not bring themselves to criticize the Nazi extermination of Europe's Jews. Some students expressed personal distaste for what the Nazis did. But they were not willing to say that the Nazis were wrong, since no culture can be judged from the outside and no individual can challenge the moral worldview of another."[2] As many as one in five students couldn't bring themselves to identify the wholesale slaughter of innocent people as *wrong*. Why? Because that would be "judgmental." We can't condemn Nazis unless we *are* Nazis. The devil must be snickering, because he's managed to confuse us on the issue of morality. Not only have we questioned God's role as our Creator, we've also begun to question the wisdom of His government.

Notice how Jesus weighs in on this issue: " 'Not everyone who says to Me, "Lord, Lord," shall enter the kingdom of heaven,

2. John Leo, "Professors Who See No Evil," *U.S. News & World Report,* July 22, 2002, http://www.usnews.com/usnews/opinion/articles/020122/ archive_022041.htm.

but he who does the will of My Father in heaven. Many will say to Me in that day, "Lord, Lord, have we not prophesied in Your name, cast out demons in Your name, and done many wonders in Your name?" And then I will declare to them, "I never knew you; depart from Me, you who practice *lawlessness!*" ' " (Matthew 7:21–23).

The final generation on planet Earth will face a moral crisis. Paul said that they will profess a form of godliness but deny God's power (see 2 Timothy 3:5). Jesus said that many people will call Him "Lord," but at the same time, will ultimately reject what He stands for. People want to be religious, but they don't want to have it impinge on their lifestyles. Following Lucifer's example, they have chosen *lawlessness* as a lifestyle.

On the other side of the issue, there are people who have God's name written in their foreheads. They "follow the Lamb wherever He goes." The Bible identifies them very clearly. "Here is the patience of the saints; here are those who keep the commandments of God and the faith of Jesus" (Revelation 14:12).

Apparently, God's last-day faithful people won't be hard to pick out of a crowd. They don't walk fifteen feet behind God, pretending not to be related. They walk right beside Him, because their allegiance to the Creator is obvious and determined.

Chapter Six

Shall We Sin?

When Chief Justice Roy Moore installed a large stone monument of the Ten Commandments in the rotunda of the Alabama Supreme Court in 2001—and was subsequently ordered by a federal judge to remove it—the story created a national sensation. Issues of church and state aside, many Christians were horrified by the thought that the Ten Commandments were not welcome in an American court of law. The public response confirmed what I had suspected all along: Christians have not completely forgotten the significance of God's moral law.

Even for us Christians, however, our daily lives seem to defy our apparent concern over the importance of God's commandments. At the end of the twentieth century, a Gallup poll discovered that there is " 'very little difference in the behavior of the churched and the unchurched on a wide range of items including lying, cheating, and stealing.' "[1] In other words, while we claim that the moral foundation of our civilization is based on God's moral code, our own lives apparently are not. I strongly suspect this inconsistency has something to do with the reason so many people refuse to take Christianity seriously. They simply can't see that following Jesus actually makes a difference in practical terms.

So where did Christians lose sight of God's moral requirements?

---

1. Quoted in Ray Comfort, *The Way of the Master* (Wheaton, Ill.: Tyndale House, 2004), 6.

How did we come to the conclusion that the way we live is not important? I believe it stems from a misunderstanding of the plan of salvation. According to the Bible, we have been saved by grace. Paul says, "For by grace you have been saved through faith, and that not of yourselves; it is the gift of God, not of works, lest anyone should boast" (Ephesians 2:8, 9).

There is nothing a sinful human being can do to earn his or her salvation. If you want to be in the kingdom of heaven, you have only one choice: you need to repent of sin and accept the gift of salvation provided by the sacrifice of Christ. Unfortunately, some Christians have taken this to mean that because our works cannot earn our salvation, our works count for nothing. But the very next verse utterly refutes this misunderstanding. Paul immediately says, "For we are His workmanship, created in Christ Jesus for good works, which God prepared beforehand that we should walk in them" (verse 10).

Living in harmony with God's moral principles was necessary *before* the human race ever fell into sin. It's not a method of earning salvation; it's the natural state of existence for people who live in harmony with God. We were *created* for good works!

Tragically, however, the idea that our works do not matter has become pervasive in modern Christian thinking. Of course, few Christians would argue that we are free to sin. But the seeds of that notion are present in much Christian writing today. For example, consider this passage from a popular book on Bible prophecy: "When He as God's only begotten Son gave Himself to die on that cross for the 'sins of the whole world,' He ended the age of law and introduced the age of grace. From that time on, individuals have been able to be eternally saved 'through faith' by repenting of their sins and calling on Christ to save them. That is why it is called the 'age of grace.' "[2] At first glance, this statement makes perfect sense. Are we saved through faith? Absolutely. Do

---

2. Tim LaHaye and Jerry B. Jenkins, *Are We Living in the End Times?* (Wheaton, Ill.: Tyndale House, 2001), 8.

we live in an age of grace? No question about it. Did God's method of saving people change at the Cross? *Not so fast!*

Read the statement again, very carefully. It suggests that prior to Calvary, God had a different set of requirements than He did afterward. It leaves you with the impression that people were theoretically able to find salvation through *obedience* to God's law prior to Christ's sacrifice (but failed to do so), and that salvation then became a matter of *grace* when He died. In some circles, this perspective has come to be known as *dispensationalism,* because it emphasizes different dispensations in God's plan to save humanity.

Even though I suspect that the author of that statement, a faithful Christian man, would likely shudder at the thought that anybody has ever been saved by obedience to God's law, the thought is nonetheless present in what he wrote. So let's address a fundamental question: has God really employed two different methods of salvation at different times?

Absolutely not. Many people feel there is a dramatic shift from "works" to "grace" between the Old and New Testaments, emphasized by Paul's statement that under the New Testament, " 'The just shall live by faith' " (Romans 1:17). What most people fail to realize is that Paul is actually quoting from the Old Testament here—from the prophet Habakkuk. Habakkuk wrote, " 'But the just shall live by his faith' " (Habakkuk 2:4).

All believers, in every age, have been saved by their faith in what God can do for them. No one has *ever* earned salvation through his or her works. Paul argues this very eloquently in his masterpiece on the subject of salvation—the book of Romans. Pay careful attention to what he says: "For if Abraham was justified by works, he has something to boast about, but not before God. For what does the Scripture say? 'Abraham believed God, and it was accounted to him for righteousness' " (Romans 4:2, 3). Paul makes it quite clear that Abraham—an Old Testament character—was *not* justified by works. He was accepted by God and considered to be righteous because of his *faith.* Read the eleventh chapter of

Hebrews, and you'll see that what God prized most about Old Testament believers was their explicit faith in Him.

Old Testament believers didn't have the benefit of knowing the story of the Cross, because the events at Calvary had not yet taken place. Yet they still operated by faith, using the sacrificial system to demonstrate their faith that the Messiah would come. Each sacrificial lamb was a symbol of faith in Christ, so that when John the Baptist first laid eyes on Jesus, he declared, " 'Behold! The Lamb of God who takes away the sin of the world!' " (John 1:29).

No one in the Old Testament was actually saved by a sacrificial animal. In fact, the book of Hebrews tells us "it is not possible that the blood of bulls and goats could take away sins" (Hebrews 10:4). Each time an Israelite offered a sacrifice, it was an act of faith, a public statement of belief that the Messiah was coming to deal with the sin problem. It had nothing to do with earning salvation through human efforts.

Modern Christians commonly stress that when Jesus died on the cross, the "law" became unnecessary. Is there support in the Bible for this claim? It depends on what you mean by the "law."

In the Old Testament, we find more than just one law. On the one hand, there is God's *moral* law, the Ten Commandments. It is a list of moral precepts, such as "you shall not kill," and "you shall not commit adultery." God wrote this law with His own finger on two tables of stone, and it was placed inside the ark of the covenant (see Exodus 31:18; Deuteronomy 10:3–5).

On the other hand, there is also a *ceremonial* law, which is often referred to as the "Law of Moses." It is a detailed set of instructions describing how sacrificial services were to be carried out in the sanctuary. Of course, when Christ died at the cross, this sacrificial system was no longer needed, because the very thing it foreshadowed had come to pass. At the very moment Christ breathed His last, an unseen hand reached into the temple in Jerusalem and tore in two the veil in the sanctuary (see Matthew 27:51). By this act, God Himself declared the sacrificial system obsolete at the death of Christ.

The moral law, on the other hand, is just as important and necessary as ever. It clearly defines right and wrong. In fact, it defines sin for us: "sin is the transgression of the law" (1 John 3:4, KJV). To suggest that Christ abolished God's moral law creates a logical absurdity. He came to deal with our sin problem, which was a result of transgressing God's law. If the moral law has been abolished, sin itself must have come to a halt at the cross of Christ—and if that's the case, no one since that time has actually needed a Savior!

If you look carefully at what Jesus taught, you'll discover He never entertained any thought of abolishing God's moral law: " 'For assuredly, I say to you, till heaven and earth pass away, one jot or one tittle will by no means pass from the law till all is fulfilled. Whoever therefore breaks one of the least of these commandments, and teaches men so, shall be called least in the kingdom of heaven; but whoever does and teaches them, he shall be called great in the kingdom of heaven' " (Matthew 5:18, 19).

God's moral law *can't* be abolished. Why? It reveals His character, and that never changes. When God says, "You shall not kill," He's telling us something important about Himself—He values life. When He says, "Do not steal" and "Do not bear false witness," He's telling us that He's honest. The Ten Commandment moral law is a picture of God.

That's why the devil objects to it. He realizes that anyone who studies God's moral principles carefully is going to come to the conclusion that God is loving, merciful, and just. The devil isn't just trying to make us commit evil deeds; he's trying to make us forget the very character of God. He's trying to keep God from writing His name in our foreheads.

The Bible tells us that when we accept Christ, we become a "new creation" (2 Corinthians 5:17). God transforms our character so that it begins to harmonize with His own. He writes His name in our foreheads. " 'This is the covenant that I will make with them after those days, says the LORD: I will put My laws into their hearts, and in their minds I will write them,' then He adds, 'Their sins and their lawless deeds I will remember no more' " (Hebrews 10:16, 17).

What does God write in our minds? His laws! What do His laws reveal? His character! What do God's last-day people have written on their foreheads? God's name! What is the significance of God's name? It represents His character!

When someone is truly in a relationship with God, it shows in his or her behavior. We become more like Christ with each passing day. We begin to hate the things we used to love, and we begin to love the things we used to hate. We are utterly transformed. Listen carefully to what God says about those who know Him: "Now by this we know that we know Him, if we keep His commandments. He who says, 'I know Him,' and does not keep His commandments, is a liar, and the truth is not in him" (1 John 2:3, 4).

It is precisely on this point that we find the biggest inconsistency in modern Christian thinking. We practically riot in the streets when unbelievers campaign to remove a stone monument to the Ten Commandments from the rotunda of a courthouse. But in our daily lives, we utterly fail to keep them. Ask yourself: which is a more persuasive argument in favor of God's government—a monument in a courthouse or a human life utterly transformed by the power of God?

Personally, I think it's a shame that Western civilization has come to the point that we feel the need to remove a copy of the Ten Commandments from public view. The bigger tragedy, however, has been the quiet but steady removal of God's moral principles from our hearts. It should come as no surprise, however, because the devil's most intense anger is poured out on those who choose to live in harmony with God: "And the dragon was enraged with the woman, and he went to make war with the rest of her offspring, who keep the commandments of God and have the testimony of Jesus Christ" (Revelation 12:17).

The devil hates those who have the Father's name emblazoned in their foreheads, because they are proving him to be a liar. They're proving—in day-to-day life—that it pays to follow God and take Him at His word. And if we Christians would continue to live publicly by the principles of God's government, the whole world would soon see that God really is love.

It's not a matter of earning your salvation; it's simply a matter of love and loyalty. Those who keep God's commandments are declaring to the world that they still believe in the government of God. They may have sinned, but they trust God's provision for them, and they choose to cast their lot with the Creator. " 'If you love Me,' " Jesus said, " 'keep My commandments' " (John 14:15).

Chapter Seven

But Wait a Minute . . .

Before I move on, it's probably important to address a few common misunderstandings about God's Ten Commandment law. Scores of biblical passages confirm the Christian's obligation—and desire—to live in harmony with it, but there are a couple of passages that have been twisted from their context to give the impression that God's moral law has been abolished. Let's take a look at them.

1. "Therefore we conclude that a man is justified by faith apart from the deeds of the law" (Romans 3:28). This is an entirely true statement, of course. No one can be justified (made right with God) through obedience to God's law. Obedience was a bare minimum requirement *before* human beings sinned, and no amount of obedience is going to make up for the fact that we have broken God's law. That would be like a judge pardoning a murderer because he promises not to kill anyone else! The moral debt we incur by sin is not solved by our future obedience.

Some people have taken this verse to mean that God no longer requires us to obey His moral law. The context of the passage, however, doesn't allow for this understanding. Just a few verses later, Paul writes, "Do we then make void the law through faith? Certainly not! On the contrary, we establish the law" (verse 31).

God's forgiveness doesn't abolish His law. On the contrary, the fact that *forgiveness* is the only solution for our sin problem underlines the permanent nature of God's moral principles. God is the same "yesterday, today, and forever" (Hebrews 13:8). He can no more change His moral law than He can change Himself. Paul clearly states that the arrangement for our salvation only serves to confirm God's law.

2. *"Sin shall not have dominion over you, for you are not under law but under grace" (Romans 6:14).* This verse easily qualifies as one of the most misunderstood and misquoted passages in the Bible. It has been suggested that this verse proves God abolished His moral law at the Cross, introducing the era of grace as opposed to the era of law. If you stop to think about it, such a conclusion doesn't even make sense. If God has abolished His moral law and it no longer exists, then no one can break it. And if no one has broken God's law, then no one has sinned (see 1 John 3:4), and no one needs God's grace! That's obviously nonsense.

Some years ago, I was in a hurry to get to the hospital, because a woman I knew was gravely ill, and I wanted to pray with her before it was too late. My foot was very heavy on the accelerator, and I was driving well over the speed limit. Not wanting to get caught, I used back roads. Unfortunately, the police had also decided to use back roads that day! As I rounded a corner, I saw a couple of officers with a radar gun. Instinctively, my foot moved to the brake, and before they could get a reading, I was well under the speed limit. I knew I was safe.

As soon as I drove past them, however, a third officer jumped out into the road and stopped me. He waved me into a driveway and stuck his head in my open window. "I'll bet you're wondering why I stopped you," he said.

"I know I wasn't speeding, so that can't be it!"

"No," he said, smiling. "You weren't speeding. But do me a favor and look out your window."

I obeyed and discovered that my seat belt was hanging out the door! "Wow," I said. "What can I say? Guilty as charged!"

"I appreciate your honesty," he said, "but you should understand that I practice absolutely no leniency when it comes to seat belts."

"That's OK," I replied, eager to get going. "I really don't have any excuse. But would you mind writing my ticket quickly, because I'm in a hurry to get to the hospital!"

At that moment, I was *under the law.* I had broken the law and deserved to pay the penalty. But then something very strange happened. Out of the corner of his eye, the officer suddenly noticed a decal in the corner of my back window that entitled me to park at the hospital for free.

"What's that?" he asked, pointing to the decal. "Are you a doctor? Is this some sort of medical emergency?"

"No," I replied, "I'm not a doctor." (To be honest, if I've ever been tempted to lie, it was right at that moment!)

"Do you have some sort of a medical exemption from wearing a seat belt?" Again, I replied in the negative. I didn't even know such a thing existed.

"Well then, why do you have that decal?"

"I'm a pastor."

Suddenly, his face fell. "Man," he said. "I don't know if I can give a ticket to a *pastor.*"

In my mind, I pictured my friend expiring while the officer—clearly still influenced by the superstition of the Dark Ages—wrestled with the possible spiritual consequences of offending a man of the cloth. "Please," I pleaded, "you can do this! *Really.* Go ahead and write me up."

He lowered his ticket book and smiled. "Listen," he said, "I know I can trust you to wear that seat belt from now on. Get out of here."

Now everything had changed. A moment earlier, I was *under the law,* because I had broken it and deserved to pay the penalty. Now I was under grace, because I had received a pardon I didn't deserve! Of course, that doesn't mean that I am now forever exempt from having to observe the rules of the road. In fact, my pardon should make me all the more careful to keep them.

Take another look at what Paul says in this passage. We are

not under the law, but under grace. We have all broken God's moral law, because the Bible states quite clearly that "all have sinned and fall short of the glory of God" (Romans 3:23). According to 1 John 1:8, "If we say that we have no sin, we deceive ourselves, and the truth is not in us." The sin problem is universal; we've all broken God's law. And the penalty for sin, according to the Bible, is *death* (see Romans 6:23). If you think about it, death is really the logical consequence for cutting yourself off from the Creator, who is the Source of all life. We are all *under the law.*

In Christ, however, God has made provision for the forgiveness of sinners. "If we confess our sins," the Bible says in 1 John 1:9, "He is faithful and just to forgive us our sins and to cleanse us from all unrighteousness." Paul puts it very eloquently: "But God demonstrates His own love toward us, in that while we were still sinners, Christ died for us. Much more then, having now been justified by His blood, we shall be saved from wrath through Him" (Romans 5:8, 9).

We have been given a pardon we do not deserve. No longer under the condemnation of God's law, we are now *under grace.* Does that remove the necessity of living in harmony with God's moral law? Of course not. Christians are not free to murder, steal, and commit adultery. On the contrary, they are quite happy to live in harmony with God's law *because* He has treated them so graciously. In fact, immediately after stating that we are under grace, Paul makes this statement in the next chapter: "What then? Shall we sin because we are not under law but under grace? Certainly not!" (Romans 6:15).

What is the purpose of God's law? According to James, the moral law is like a mirror. It shows us our true condition (see James 1:23–25). When we examine God's moral requirements, we can see very clearly just how far short of God's glory our own characters fall. The Ten Commandments show us that God is honest—and that we are not. They show us that God values life far more than we do. They point out every flaw and defect in our sinful hearts. And if we're listening to God's voice, and we realize just how bad our situation really is, that same law will drive us to Christ for help because we see there is nothing we can do to remedy the situation ourselves. "The law of the LORD is perfect," says Psalm 19:7, "converting the soul."

There are only two kinds of people in this world—those whose hearts belong to the Creator, and those whose hearts belong to fallen angels. Everyone is a sinner, but each person's allegiance will determine how he or she responds to sin. It's a little like the difference between a pig and a lamb. Both animals might slip and fall in the mud, but they will respond differently. A pig wallows in the mud, enjoying every minute he spends in the filth. A lamb, on the other hand, promptly jumps up and runs to the shepherd for a bath.

There's more going on in our world than first meets the eye. The devil isn't just trying to make people do bad things; he's trying to scrub the memory of the Creator from our minds. He wants to use human beings, created in the very image of God, to discredit the Creator's government. In the end, God has a people whose minds are made up, who are determined to belong entirely to Him.

Chapter Eight

One Day Is as Good as Another—Right?

As the moral foundation of Western civilization threatens to crumble, not all is lost. The knowledge of the Creator has not been unalterably removed from human memory—God has seen to that. There is a powerful drive in the human heart—a homing beacon, if you will—that draws and woos us back to Him.

Consider the very fact that we are disappointed with the state of human existence. We hate our own pain and suffering because it makes us uncomfortable. But why does the suffering of *others* bother us? How do we know there's something wrong with life here on this earth, unless we have a distant memory of a better existence? With what are we comparing the apparent shortcomings of our world?

Why does *death* bother us? If it's really just part of the normal cycle of life, why do we fight so hard against it? We spend untold millions each year to battle disease and extend the human life span, because something in our hearts tells us death is *wrong*. Even though our experience on this planet is limited to a handful of decades, our minds seem as though they've been programmed to go on forever. We struggle to imagine a planet that goes on without us. We quietly lament that life offers more experiences than we have time to participate in.

I often open Google Earth on my computer's desktop and start the planet slowly spinning so I can watch it while I work. With each revolution of the planet, I see a growing list of places I will never have the time or resources to visit—and suddenly, I feel cheated by the whole experience of life and death. Why do I have an inborn sense of eternity that defies human experience?

There's an unusual passage in the Bible that holds the key to understanding these mysteries. Ecclesiastes 3:11 tells us that God "has put eternity in their hearts." Even though our rebellion against His government has brought death to the human experience, He hasn't allowed our memory of Eden to perish. He keeps it alive, using it to woo us back into a saving relationship with Him that will end with eternity—and the Garden—restored to us in full.

Witness the strange case of Paul's visit to the city of Lystra. After Paul and Barnabas healed a man who had been crippled since birth, the citizens of the city assumed the two men must be incarnations of the Roman gods Jupiter and Mercury. They quickly made preparations to worship the apostles. In fact, they were so convinced of the men's deity that Paul and Barnabas were barely able to persuade them to stop (see Acts 14:18). In essence, the apostles told the Lystrians that there was no excuse for worshiping a mere human being. Why? Notice their argument:

> But when the apostles Barnabas and Paul heard this, they tore their clothes and ran in among the multitude, crying out and saying, "Men, why are you doing these things? We also are men with the same nature as you, and preach to you that you should turn from these useless things to the living God, who made the heaven, the earth, the sea, and all things that are in them, who in bygone generations allowed all nations to walk in their own ways. Nevertheless He did not leave Himself without witness, in that He did good, gave us rain from heaven and fruitful seasons, filling our hearts with food and gladness" (Acts 14:14–17).

"You have no excuse for this," Paul said, "because you have plenty of evidence at hand to remind you of the Creator." Think about that carefully. It means that *even without a Bible,* everyone on earth has enough evidence to rediscover the Creator. Even though God has allowed rebellious human beings to go their own way, He has left enough pointers along life's path to help us rediscover Him. Paul makes the same point in the book of Romans: "For since the creation of the world His invisible attributes are clearly seen, being understood by the things that are made, even His eternal power and Godhead, so that they are without excuse, because, although they knew God, they did not glorify Him as God, nor were thankful, but became futile in their thoughts, and their foolish hearts were darkened" (Romans 1:20, 21).

Paul argues that in order to be unaware of the Creator, you have to *do so on purpose.* You have to ignore the evidence. History is filled with people who rediscovered the story of the Creator quite apart from a visit by Christian missionaries. Take, for example, the case of Pachacuti, the illustrious ninth king of the Inca Empire. Most of his life, he worshiped the Inca sun god, Inti—but careful reasoning began to tell him he might be worshiping a false god. If the sun were truly a god, why did it never intervene in the affairs of human beings? And why did it seem to follow a prescribed course across the heavens every single day? Would it really be possible for a genuine god to be obscured by a tiny little cloud? Gradually, Pachacuti came to the conclusion that the sun was not a god at all.

If the sun weren't a god, however, who was he supposed to worship? He began to research the history of his people, and became greatly interested in a god by the name of *Viracocha.* His own father had switched to the worship of Viracocha some years earlier, becoming so devoted that he changed his own name to match that of his new god. Viracocha was described as the all-powerful creator of the universe who himself had no beginning and manifested himself as a triune being. Pachacuti called a meeting of the highest religious officials in his empire and attempted to persuade them to return to the worship of the creator, with limited success.

Paul was right. There's a large enough body of evidence available to *anyone* for God to pull him or her back in His direction. In fact, Paul describes such people—those whose hearts are true to the Creator but do not have access to the Scriptures—as having the law written in their hearts: "(for when Gentiles, who do not have the law, by nature do the things in the law, these, although not having the law, are a law to themselves, who show the work of the law written in their hearts, their conscience also bearing witness, and between themselves their thoughts accusing or else excusing them) in the day when God will judge the secrets of men by Jesus Christ, according to my gospel" (Romans 2:14–16).

Such people might never lay eyes on a copy of the Ten Commandments, but God is entirely reasonable. He knows what people have—or have not—had access to through the course of their lives. (As Paul preached to a crowd of idol worshipers in Athens, he pointed out that God "winks" at our times of ignorance, but calls us to repentance when we have more knowledge [see Acts 17:30]). When a person lives up to the knowledge he has and follows the evidence placed at his disposal, God counts him as having been loyal to Him on the "day when God will judge the secrets of men by Jesus Christ" (Romans 2:16).

In the final moments before Christ returns, however, God ratchets up His campaign to win back the citizens of our fallen planet. An urgent message is carried to the farthest reaches of the globe, calling for people of every conceivable background to return to a worship of the Creator. The apostle John describes what he saw in vision: "Then I saw another angel flying in the midst of heaven, having the everlasting gospel to preach to those who dwell on the earth—to every nation, tribe, tongue, and people—saying with a loud voice, 'Fear God and give glory to Him, for the hour of His judgment has come; and worship Him who made heaven and earth, the sea and springs of water' " (Revelation 14:6, 7).

It's astounding how the language of this pressing call—He "made heaven and earth, the sea and springs of water"—mirrors the language used throughout the Bible to describe God's worthiness as the object of our worship. More specifically, it's astounding how this passage mirrors the Sabbath commandment: " 'For in six days the LORD made the heavens and the earth, the sea, and all that is in them, and rested the seventh day. Therefore the LORD blessed the Sabbath day and hallowed it' " (Exodus 20:11).

Let's review a few key facts in the story of Lucifer's fall. His crime against God was one of "iniquity," or lawlessness (see Ezekiel 28:15).[1] He stood in direct contrast to the righteous and moral character of God. He longed to occupy God's throne and be worshiped in a manner fitting only for the Creator (see Isaiah 14:13, 14).

Is it a coincidence that the one commandment that is specifically centered on God's right to our worship is the commandment the whole world seems to have forgotten? Imagine: if every single week the whole world had continued to observe God's Sabbath—to cease ordinary activities and worship God as the Creator—what are the odds that we would have been so ready to adopt alternate theories of human origins? Why is the theory of evolution such a hot topic? Why are both sides of the debate so passionate about it?

It's because they echo the two sides portrayed in the final events described by the book of Revelation. On the one side, there is Lucifer, who craves worship. In Revelation 13, he provides compelling alternatives to the worship of the one true Creator God, even *forcing* people to worship his false system when gentle persuasion fails. On the other side, there is the final warning message in Revelation 14 that goes to all the world, pleading with humanity

---

1. The original Hebrew word is '*evel,* which denotes "injustice." The same word is used to describe a judge who disregards justice (see Leviticus 19:15, 35) or a businessman who is dishonest (see Deuteronomy 25:13–16). God's justice and righteousness are said to be in direct opposition to this characteristic (see Deuteronomy 32:4).

to return to the Creator—to worship Him who made the earth and sea and sky.

Let's take it a step further. When I was in the fifth grade, a new kid joined my class. He was smarter than most of the rest of us, as evidenced by the fact that he had skipped a grade to join us. He and I became good friends. One day he was at my house playing. "Shawn," he said, suddenly, "why does your family go to church on Sunday?"

"What do you mean," I asked, more than a little confused. "What day do you go to church?"

"Saturday," he replied, as if it were the most natural thing in the world.

"Saturday?" I had never heard anything so strange in all my ten years. (Bear in mind that I grew up in a small northern Canadian town, and to my knowledge, we had no practicing Jews living there.) "Who in the world goes to church on Saturday? What kind of goofy church do you go to?"

Sensing that he was up against a pigheaded blockhead who wasn't willing to listen (he was right), he dropped the argument, and we went on playing. More than a decade later, God revived the question in my mind. *Why exactly* did *I go to church on Sunday?*

There's an old legend about a Russian tsar who was walking around the palace grounds one day when he suddenly noticed a lonely guard standing in a remote corner of the property. He asked the guard why he was standing there and what he was guarding. The guard had no idea. "I don't know," he answered. "All I know is that it is my duty to stand here."

Dissatisfied with the answer, the tsar began to inquire further among his staff. For as long as anyone could remember, guards had been assigned to watch the same spot. No one knew why. The captain of the guard was asked to investigate; and after a lengthy search, he found the answer. More than a hundred years earlier, Catherine the Great had planted a favorite rosebush on the spot and ordered it to be carefully guarded so that no one would damage it. The rosebush had long since died, but no one had thought to rescind the orders to guard its location. For more than a century, the palace guard had been watching *nothing*!

There are those who doubt the authenticity of this story, but it serves to illustrate an important point. There are scores of things we do in life for which the original reason has been lost sight of. Why, for example, is a croissant crescent-shaped? As it turns out, when the Turks invaded the city of Budapest in the seventeenth century, they were soundly defeated. To celebrate, local bakers made pastries in the shape of a crescent, the symbol of Islam. To this day, the pastry continues to be crescent-shaped, but few people remember why.

So why do we worship God on Sunday? The Genesis account tells us that God blessed and sanctified the *seventh* day of the week. The fourth commandment reiterates that fact. Check your dictionary and calendar, however. Sunday is not the seventh day of the week, it is the *first*. So how did Christians come to treat the first day of the week as holy?

I was told, growing up, that the Sabbath was for the Jews, and that Christians observed the first day of the week in honor of Christ's resurrection. Upon investigating this further, I discovered a number of problems with that statement. First, the Sabbath existed centuries before any Jews occupied the face of the earth. Adam and Eve were not Jews, and yet the seventh day had already been blessed and sanctified by God at Creation. Second, Jesus Himself stated that the " 'Sabbath was made for *man*' " (Mark 2:27, emphasis supplied). Notice, He didn't say that the Sabbath was made for *Jews*. God intended the blessing of the Sabbath for all humanity. Furthermore, nowhere does the Bible indicate any change of the day of worship from the seventh to the first day of the week. (More on this in a moment.)

Check the biblical record carefully, and you'll notice something amazing. The Sabbath has always been—and always will be—the seventh day of the week. It was instituted by the Creator Himself in the Garden of Eden (see Genesis 2:1–3). It was in existence prior to the Israelites receiving a copy of God's law at Mount Sinai, as demonstrated in God's instruction to Israel for gathering manna. God told the people, " 'Six days you shall gather it, but on the seventh day, the Sabbath, there will be none' " (Exodus 16:26).

We find the seventh-day Sabbath emblazoned in the heart of God's moral law as He copied it onto tables of stone with His own finger (see Exodus 20:8–11; 24:12; Deuteronomy 5:22). The Israelites continued to observe the Sabbath (with brief periods of unfaithfulness) until the time of Christ, when it was clearly still in effect.

There is no record in the Bible of Jesus changing the day of worship, either. In Luke's Gospel, we discover that Jesus—as we might expect—observed the Sabbath as He was growing up: "So He came to Nazareth, where He had been brought up. And as His custom was, He went into the synagogue on the Sabbath day, and stood up to read" (Luke 4:16). Did He change the day of worship later on? The Bible makes no mention of Him doing so. In fact, there is clear evidence that Jesus didn't anticipate a change in the Sabbath even after He returned to heaven. Pay careful attention to the details in Matthew, where Jesus accurately predicted the destruction of the Jerusalem temple by the Romans roughly forty years after His crucifixion. What did He say? " 'And pray that your flight may not be in winter or on the Sabbath' " (Matthew 24:20).

If Christ had planned to abolish the Sabbath or change it to another day, this would have been the ideal opportunity to mention it. He doesn't. Apparently, He never expected a change in the day of worship. It's not hard to figure out why. If God's law is a reflection of His character, it is not subject to change. He is the same yesterday, today, and forever (see Hebrews 13:8). So is His law.

Perhaps the disciples changed the day of worship. This is the reason I was given for Sunday worship when I was a kid; I was told that the disciples replaced the Sabbath with worship on the first day of the week to create a permanent memorial to the death, burial, and resurrection of Christ. You can imagine my consternation when I couldn't find any evidence of this act in the Bible! After the death of Jesus and His burial in the tomb, one of the first things the disciples did was observe the Sabbath "according to the commandment" (Luke 23:56). Of course, they wouldn't have known that Christ was going to rise from the grave at that point, so we can theoretically excuse this one last Sabbath observance before the Resurrection. The rest of the Bible, however, provides absolutely no evidence that the disciples changed the Sabbath. In fact, it gives a number of clear examples where they continued to observe it. Let's look at some of these. "But when they departed from Perga, they came to Antioch in Pisidia, and went into the synagogue on the Sabbath day and sat down" (Acts 13:14).

I've heard people try to explain that the only reason Paul was preaching in church on the Sabbath was because he wanted to reach to the Jews, and that's where they were to be found on that day. The major problem with that understanding is found a little later in the same story: "So when the Jews went out of the synagogue, the Gentiles begged that these words might be preached to them the next Sabbath. . . . On the next Sabbath almost the whole city came together to hear the word of God" (verses 42, 44).

This would have been the ideal opportunity for Paul to tell the Gentiles that (a) the Sabbath had been abolished, or (b) it had been moved to the first day of the week. You'll notice he says nothing of the sort.

Keep reading the story, and you'll find something interesting. Paul wasn't observing the Sabbath simply because he was eager to keep the Jewish crowd appeased. In fact, he makes a very bold statement in the following verses indicating that he had given up on the Jewish population of that city and was now primarily concerned with the Gentiles! (See verses 45–48.)

Acts 18:4 tells us that in the city of Corinth, Paul "reasoned in the synagogue every Sabbath, and persuaded both Jews and Greeks." He was in that city for a year and a half (see verse 11), which makes for a total of seventy-eight Sabbaths. Surely, if Paul intended to let his followers know that the Sabbath had been changed or abolished, that would have been enough time to do it. But Paul is silent on that subject, because the Bible never mentions a change.

Even when there wasn't a synagogue available, Paul continued to recognize the Sabbath: "And on the Sabbath day we went out of the city to the riverside, where prayer was customarily made; and we sat down and spoke to the women who met there" (Acts 16:13). I have searched the Bible in vain for any mention of a change in the day set aside for the worship of God. It simply isn't there. The Bible points to several memorials to the death and resurrection of Christ—the Communion service (see 1 Corinthians 11:24, 25) and the rite of baptism (see Romans 6:4–6). A change of the seventh-day Sabbath is never mentioned.

Let me pause for a moment and share something interesting that I discovered along the way. Many people go through life under the impression that somehow God the Father and God the Son are at odds with each other. The Father, as it has been explained on many occasions, is a God of law and war. The Son, on the other hand, is a God of love and mercy. Vivid descriptions of Christ pleading with the Father to not destroy the human race have poured out of many pulpits over the centuries, but it's a gross mischaracterization of God. Jesus explained that the " 'the Father Himself loves you' " (John 16:27). The most famous verse in the Bible tells us that " 'God so loved the world that He gave His only begotten Son' " (John 3:16).

The plan of salvation is a cooperative effort. Why do I mention this? Many people mentally separate the Old and New Testaments into two separate dispensations, as I've already pointed out. The Old Testament, it is assumed, was a dispensation of law, in contrast to the New Testament, which is assumed to be a dispensation of grace. We have already laid to rest the notion that Old Testament believers were saved according to a different plan than us, but allow me to elaborate a little. Because of this misguided understanding of God—a severe Father overseeing the Old Testament and a merciful Son overseeing the New—some people have subconsciously used this model to make sense of a change in the day of worship. If circumstances and even salvation are so radically different in the Old Testament compared to the New, then why might there not be a different day of worship in the New Testament? Few people have expressed this thought explicitly, but I suspect it forms one of the foundations for the comfort we have felt in observing an alternate Sabbath.

What *has* been stated many times is the idea that we honor Sunday in place of the Sabbath because of our desire to honor Christ. After all, people argue, Sunday is the "Lord's Day."

Right? Don't be so sure.

Some of the early church fathers referred to Sunday as the "Lord's Day," but not until many years after Christ's ascension into heaven. The Bible never does so. In fact, the *only* reference to the "Lord's Day" found in Scripture is in the book of Revelation: "I was in the Spirit on the Lord's Day, and I heard behind me a loud voice, as of a trumpet, saying, 'I am the Alpha and the Omega, the First and the Last' " (Revelation 1:10, 11). There is no further elaboration, no mention of which day John believed to be the "Lord's Day." The rest of the Bible, however, makes it abundantly clear which day *God* calls His day:

"For the Son of Man is Lord even of the Sabbath" (Matthew 12:8).

" 'Hallow My Sabbaths, and they will be a sign between Me and you, that you may know that I am the LORD your God' " (Ezekiel 20:20).

" 'But the seventh day is the Sabbath of the LORD your God' " (Exodus 20:10).

Now let's go back and think about the false dichotomy some people make between God the Father (presiding over the Old Testament) and God the Son (presiding over the New). In their desire to honor Christ with the first day of the week, many people fail to remember that *He* is the Creator! Consider these important passages:

All things were made through Him, and without Him nothing was made that was made (John 1:3).

For by Him all things were created that are in heaven and that are on earth, visible and invisible, whether thrones or dominions or principalities or powers. All things were created through Him and for Him (Colossians 1:16).

God, who at various times and in various ways spoke in time past to the fathers by the prophets, has in these last days spoken to us by His Son, whom He has appointed heir of all things, through whom also He made the worlds (Hebrews 1:1, 2).

Think this through very carefully. If Christ is the Creator, what day best honors His memory? The very day He established at Creation—the seventh-day Sabbath. I suppose the appropriate question might be: Does it matter? What difference does it make? Isn't one day as good as another, as long as you set aside one day in seven?

It's a nice thought and one that I hear often, but there is no biblical evidence to support it. When I first met my wife, it didn't take long for me to fall head over heels in love with her, and I'm happy to report that I feel only more strongly about her with each passing year. Let's suppose, for the sake of argument, that my wife has six sisters. After a long courtship (we dated for more than four years), I finally work up the courage to ask her father the age-old question: May I marry your daughter? To my delight, he says Yes.

On the big day, I'm as nervous as you'd expect any groom to be. After what seems like an eternity of standing on the platform, I hear the music suddenly change; I see the doors at the back of the church swing open. My future father-in-law is walking a veiled bride down the aisle. The minister leads us through the ceremony, and at its conclusion, after pronouncing us man and wife, he informs me that I may kiss my bride.

You can imagine my horror when I lift the veil to discover I've just married the *wrong sister*. Furious, I turn to my father-in-law, "What's going on? This isn't *Jean!*"

To which he shrugs his shoulders dispassionately and mutters, "What's the difference? I've got seven daughters. One girl is as good as another." (This scenario isn't as far-fetched as it might seem. Don't forget that this actually happened to Jacob!)

One girl is *not* as good as another. We had invested *four years* in a relationship, and I wanted to marry the girl I love. Read the biblical account carefully. One day is *not* as good as another. God did three specific things on the seventh day: He rested, He blessed the day, and He sanctified it (see Genesis 2:1–3). All three things are repeated in the fourth commandment: " 'For in six days the LORD made the heavens and the earth, the sea, and all that is in them, and *rested* the seventh day. Therefore the LORD *blessed* the Sabbath day and *hallowed* it' " (Exodus 20:11, emphasis supplied).

He didn't do any of these things with the other six days. In fact, the fourth commandment specifically mentions that the other six days are for *working*, which is as much a part of the commandment as observing the seventh day.

"But I worship God *every* day—not just one day in seven!" I know. That was one of my first responses too, when I began learning about the importance of the seventh-day Sabbath. But think about it. Although God expects us to honor Him and maintain our relationship with Him every day of the week, He didn't create all days equal. On the seventh day, He expects us to utterly put our work aside and engage Him fully in a way that's simply not possible on the other six days, which are full of distractions. I love my wife 365 days a year, but our anniversary is special. On that day, we *celebrate*.

Of course, we still haven't answered the question: how did the day of worship become changed? Keep reading; you might be surprised!

Chapter Nine

Who Changed the Sabbath— and Why?

Let's quickly review what we studied in the last chapter. The seventh-day Sabbath has been in existence as a memorial to God's creative power since the beginning of time. Its origin is clearly explained in the story of Creation (see Genesis 2:1–3). It is found in God's Ten Commandment moral law (see Exodus 20:8–11). The nation of Israel clearly observed it throughout the Old Testament. Jesus also observed it and never anticipated that it would be changed (see Matthew 24:20; Luke 4:16). The disciples continued to observe it throughout the New Testament (see Luke 23:56; Acts 13:14, 42, 44; 16:13; 18:4).

Now, are you ready for another surprise? The Bible indicates that the Sabbath will still be in existence in the earth made new.

> "For as the new heavens and the new earth
> Which I will make shall remain before Me," says the
>   Lord,
> "So shall your descendants and your name remain.
> And it shall come to pass
> That from one New Moon to another,
> And from one Sabbath to another,
> All flesh shall come to worship before Me," says the
>   Lord (Isaiah 66:22, 23).

Let that sink in for a moment.

Some have suggested that the seventh-day Sabbath is part of the Old Testament ceremonial system that was abolished at the Cross. If that's the case, it would be the only one of the Ten Commandments to be abolished. No one suggests that the other nine aren't still in effect. Furthermore, the ceremonial law (which plainly became unnecessary after the Cross) deals with sacrifices for *sin*. The seventh-day Sabbath clearly predates sin: God blessed and sanctified the seventh-day Sabbath before Adam even had a chance to sin. Obviously, it can't be part of the ceremonial system. It wasn't instituted to foreshadow the Cross as did the sacrificial, ceremonial system; the Sabbath was established as a memorial of Creation.

And the seventh-day Sabbath will still be in effect when sin is finished. Long after Christ has returned and we are enjoying a brand-new planet, we will continue to worship God on the Sabbath, according to Isaiah.

My point? The Sabbath was clearly part of God's original plan for the human race; it would have existed even if we had never sinned.

Now put the pieces together. If the Sabbath existed *before* sin, it was in effect all the way through the time of the disciples. We have seen that it will exist *after* sin. So what are the odds that God has suspended or changed the Sabbath for just a relatively few years? Yet there's no question that the vast majority of Christian believers today are keeping the first day of the week—without a shred of biblical evidence to support it!

How is this possible? In light of what we know about the struggle for God's throne, it makes sense. God's moral law reflects His perfect character, and Lucifer is eager to distract us from understanding that, if at all possible. Furthermore, there is one law in particular that underlines God's right to be worshiped, and if any one of God's laws is going to draw the particular wrath of the devil, you'd expect it to be that one. The whole struggle in our universe finds its roots in the issue of *worship*, so you've got to expect the day set aside for the specific purpose of honoring God as the Creator might become an issue.

Let's take a closer look. As we've already discussed, there is absolutely no mention of a change in the day of worship anywhere in the Bible. The first day of the week is mentioned exactly eight times in the New Testament, but not a single one of these references indicates that God intended a change of the Sabbath. Let's look at the all the places where the New Testament refers to the first day of the week.

1. *"Then they returned and prepared spices and fragrant oils. And they rested on the Sabbath according to the commandment. Now on the first day of the week, very early in the morning, they, and certain other women with them, came to the tomb bringing the spices which they had prepared" (Luke 23:56–24:1).* If anything, this passage reinforces the Sabbath commandment. In spite of the horrific events of that day, the followers of Jesus took care to remember the Sabbath. Perhaps there's a lesson here for all of us. When life gets really, really tough, it becomes all the more important to put everything aside and *rest* in God's ability to pull us through. On this particular Sabbath, unfortunately, the disciples actually missed the point and spent the day holed up, hiding from the Jewish authorities because they were afraid they'd be the next ones to hang on a cross.

As for the first day of the week, this passage simply says the followers of Jesus returned early in the morning to embalm His body. They were, of course, utterly unaware of the Resurrection at this point. There is nothing here to suggest a change in the day of worship.

2. *"Now when the Sabbath was past, Mary Magdalene, Mary the mother of James, and Salome bought spices, that they might come and anoint Him. Very early in the morning, on the first day of the week, they came to the tomb when the sun had risen" (Mark 16:1, 2).* This passage is like the first one we looked at—it simply states that on the first day of the week, the women returned to the tomb

to finish embalming Christ's body. It is universally recognized, of course, that Christ rose on the day we now refer to as Sunday, which is still, to this day, the first day of the week. (The Jews simply numbered their days: first day, second day, etc. The sixth day was called "the preparation" in anticipation of the Sabbath, and the seventh day, of course, was called "the Sabbath.") You'll notice that this passage identifies the "Sabbath" as the day before Sunday, the first day of the week. These verses do little to suggest a change in the day of worship; in fact, if anything, they establish that the day before Sunday is the Sabbath!

3. *"Now when He rose early on the first day of the week, He appeared first to Mary Magdalene, out of whom He had cast seven demons" (Mark 16:9).* There's not much need for comment on this verse, other than to point out that it simply states Christ rose from the dead on the first day of the week. Nothing here could be even remotely used to suggest a change of the Sabbath.

4. *"On the first day of the week Mary Magdalene came to the tomb early, while it was still dark, and saw that the stone had been taken away from the tomb" (John 20:1).* Once again, this is a simple statement of chronology. In perfect harmony with the other Gospel writers, John mentions that the followers of Jesus returned to the tomb on the first day of the week. Again, there is no mention of a change in the Sabbath.

5. *"Now after the Sabbath, as the first day of the week began to dawn, Mary Magdalene and the other Mary came to see the tomb" (Matthew 28:1).* This passage is like the others we've examined. The first day of the week comes immediately *after* the day identified as the Sabbath. Once again, there is no mention of a change of the day of worship.

6. *"Then, the same day at evening, being the first day of the week, when the doors were shut where the disciples were assembled, for fear of the Jews, Jesus came and stood in the midst, and said to them, 'Peace be with you'" (John 20:19).* There's a little more to this passage than the last five we've looked at. I've heard some

people suggest that because the disciples were assembled on the "first day of the week," we have evidence of a church service on Sunday. There are two problems with that understanding.

First, at this point, the disciples had no idea that Christ had risen from the dead, so they couldn't possibly be meeting in a worship service in honor of the Resurrection. Second, the Bible tells us exactly why the disciples were gathered. It wasn't for the purpose of worship; they were hiding in fear!

Nothing in this passage even remotely suggests that God intended to shift the Sabbath from the seventh to the first day of the week.

7. *"Now concerning the collection for the saints, as I have given orders to the churches of Galatia, so you must do also: On the first day of the week let each one of you lay something aside, storing up as he may prosper, that there be no collections when I come"* (1 Corinthians 16:1, 2). These verses, of course, were written by Paul. Some have suggested that he's talking about taking up a collection during a church service on the first day of the week, but a careful reading eliminates that possibility. Historically, we know there was a famine raging in Jerusalem, which led Paul to request financial assistance for the victims. He suggests that each believer "lay something aside" on the first day of the week for the purpose of famine relief so that he doesn't have to try and scrape together money when he arrives in Corinth.

If the believers were all in church on the first day of the week, how could they "lay something aside"? The language of Paul's request indicates that they were busy working! At least eight translations of the Bible have Paul saying the Corinthians were to lay aside an offering "privately," or "at home." *The New Testament in Modern Speech,* for example, renders Paul's request like this: "On the first day of every week let each of you put on one side and store up at his home whatever gain has been granted to him."

Darby's New Translation says the same thing: "On [the] first of [the] week let each of you put by at home, laying up [in] whatever [degree] he may have prospered."

Paul is simply asking the Corinthian believers to make a point of setting something aside for famine relief at the beginning of the week. We would do well to follow suit; human nature is such that if we leave God until the end of the week, we won't likely have much to give. Likewise, the book of Proverbs advises, "Honor the LORD with your possessions, / And with the firstfruits of all your increase" (Proverbs 3:9). The general rule of Christian stewardship is to put the cause of God first. Paul is simply emphasizing this to a group of Christians who were obviously back at work on the first day of the week.

8. *"Now on the first day of the week, when the disciples came together to break bread, Paul, ready to depart the next day, spoke to them and continued his message until midnight. There were many lamps in the upper room where they were gathered together. And in a window sat a certain young man named Eutychus, who was sinking into a deep sleep. He was overcome by sleep; and as Paul continued speaking, he fell down from the third story and was taken up dead. But Paul went down, fell on him, and embracing him said, 'Do not trouble yourselves, for his life is in him.' Now when he had come up, had broken bread and eaten, and talked a long while, even till daybreak, he departed"* (Acts 20:7–11). Of all eight references to the first day of the week in the New Testament, this one probably requires the most clarification. It is often asserted that the meeting described here must have been a religious service on the first day of the week, because the "disciples came together to break bread." If this is all the evidence required to establish a new worship day, we immediately run into a problem. Acts 2:46 tells us that the disciples were in the habit of breaking bread together every day. Does that mean that *every* day of the week is now a sabbath? Of course not.

Read this story carefully. Paul is about to leave town, and the believers in Troas are having a farewell meeting with him. We're told it was the "first day of the week" and that Paul "continued his message until midnight." If so, exactly when did these events take place? Pay careful attention to the way the translators of the *New English Bible* rendered this passage: "On the Saturday night, in our assembly for the breaking of bread, Paul, who was about to leave the next day, addressed them, and went on speaking until midnight" (Acts 20:7, NEB).

If the meeting took place on the first day of the week, why do the translators of this version call it "Saturday night"? It's really quite simple. We measure days from midnight to midnight, a custom we borrowed from the Romans. The Jews, on the other hand, measured days from sunset to sunset. This is why, in the first chapter of Genesis, each of the days of Creation are described as "evening and morning." When the sun set on the seventh day of the week, the Sabbath was over and the first day of the week had begun. (Biblically, the Sabbath also begins on Friday night when the sun sets. See Leviticus 23:32.) This meeting described in Acts 20 didn't take place on a Sunday morning, as many have supposed. It actually took place on Saturday night.

When the sun came up in the morning (Sunday morning, by our modern reckoning), Paul quit speaking and set off on foot to catch a ship in Assos—a city nineteen miles away! If God had now declared Sunday to be a holy day, a nineteen-mile hike would hardly count as Sabbath rest. But regardless of *when* this meeting took place, there is still nothing at all in this passage to suggest that God intended to change His mind about the Sabbath.

So there you have it—every single mention of the first day of the week in the New Testament, and not even a hint of a change. Heavyweight religious scholar James Cardinal Gibbons agrees, "You may read the Bible from Genesis to Revelation, and you will not find a single line authorizing the sanctification of Sunday. The Scriptures enforce the religious observance of Saturday, a day which we never sanctify."[1]

1. James Cardinal Gibbons, *The Faith of Our Fathers* (Rockford, Ill.: TAN Books, 1980), 72, 73. (Originally published in 1876 by the John Murphy Company, Baltimore, Md.)

The Sign

It's crystal clear that neither Jesus or the disciples changed the day, so the questions remain: who did change it, and why did it happen? To find these answers, we have to dig into the history books.

Within a few decades after Christ's return to heaven, the Christian church was challenged by devastating persecution by the Roman Empire. This is no surprise to students of history; we have vague memories of stories of Christians being thrown to the lions. Even though the Romans officially tolerated the various religious beliefs of their subjects, they were insistent that Caesar be added to everyone's list of gods. This wasn't a problem for most religions, but for Jews and Christians, this clearly was not a possibility. God had told them, " 'You shall have no other gods before Me' " (Exodus 20:3). Unlike most of the other religious groups subjugated by the Romans, Christians and Jews were monotheists—they worshiped only *one* God, the Creator.

Of course, this drew the wrath of the devil upon these groups. While other religions were permitted a relatively peaceful existence in the empire, the Romans displayed a remarkable antipathy towards Jews and Christians. During the middle of the first century, a flood of anti-Semitic writing poured into the streets of Rome, and as persecution intensified, a number of cowardly Christians in the city sought to distance themselves from their theological cousins. They became hesitant to openly keep the Sabbath, because Sabbath observance was one of the clear identifying marks of the Jewish population.

By the second century, Christian writers such as Justin Martyr were openly condemning Sabbath observance, referring it as a "mark to single them [the Jews] out for punishment they so well deserve for their infidelities."[2]

Over time, Christians began to observe a solemn fast on the Sabbath in an attempt to distance themselves from the Jews,

2. *Dialogue With Trypho,* 21.1. From Samuele Bacchiocchi, *The Rise of Sunday Observance in Early Christianity,* in Kenneth A. Strand, ed., *The Sabbath in Scripture and History* (Washington, D.C.: Review and Herald® Publishing Assn., 1982), 137.

who routinely *celebrated* the Sabbath. Of course, those who were fasting could no longer celebrate Communion on the seventh day of the week, and eventually Christian observance of the Sabbath was dispensed with altogether in the city of Rome. Outside of the city of Rome, Christians continued to observe the Sabbath of the Creator.

The compromise of the Roman Christians didn't spare them the wrath of the empire, as any high school history student will know. Along with the Jews, the early Christian church also became the subject of intense persecution, spurred on by the emperor Nero. When Nero wanted to clear a swath of the city to make way for development, he had it set on fire. To cover up what he had done, he chose the Christians as a scapegoat, suggesting that they were responsible for the devastating inferno. Public opinion quickly turned against the followers of Christ, and it became open season on Christians. And, as you've learned in history class, it wasn't pretty. They were thrown to half-starved wild animals as a form of public entertainment and dragged behind horses through the streets of Rome until they were dead. On at least one occasion, Nero had Christians dipped in tar, hung on poles, and lit on fire to illuminate his gardens during an outdoor party. Persecution intensified for the next few centuries until it reached its apex under the brief reign of Emperor Diocletian.

Then, in A.D. 312, something happened that put a stop to it almost overnight: Emperor Constantine became a Christian. On his way to the Battle of Milvian Bridge, he claimed to experience a vision in which he saw a cross[3] superimposed on the sun and heard a voice uttering the words, *"In Hoc Signo Vinces."*[4] ("In this

---

3. To be more precise, it is claimed that he saw two letters of the Greek alphabet—a *chi* and a *rho*—that resemble an X and a P respectively. These are the first two letters in the Greek spelling of "Christ" (Χριστός), and when superimposed on each other, form a widely recognized Christian symbol.

4. This is actually the Latin version of what Constantine supposedly heard. In the original version of the story, the phrase was uttered in Greek: *"ἐν τούτωι νίκα"* ("By this, be victorious.").

sign, you will conquer.") When he subsequently won the battle and defeated Maxentius, he took his victory as a sign from the Christian God that the Roman Empire was to conduct its business under the banner of the cross.

Constantine's claim to have become a Christian is highly suspect: he waited until he was on his deathbed to be baptized, and he continued to surround himself with pagan advisors. He apparently thought of the Christian religion as nothing more than either a good luck charm or a shrewd political move. Nonetheless, his "conversion" utterly transformed the Roman Empire. With the edict of Milan in A.D. 313, Christianity was officially tolerated, and persecution against Christians came to a grinding halt. Suddenly, it became fashionable to be a Christian, and Christian churches were flooded with halfhearted "converts."

This created a more serious problem for Christians than the persecution had. Although thousands of people suddenly became Christians, their conversions were nominal, and they continued to keep their pagan traditions. In order to maintain the peace, it was suggested that overtly pagan symbols and practices be retooled to give them Christian significance. So statues of pagan gods were renamed after the apostles, and certain pagan festivals were given new, Christian meanings. Among the pagan customs that were popular at the time was a feast known as the *dies natalis Solis Invicti*—"the birthday of the Invincible Sun"—which took place on December 25 and was a celebration in honor of the highly popular sun god. The early Roman Church, of course, could not endorse pagan sun worship, so the day was recast as a celebration of the birth of Christ.[5] Of course, setting aside a day to celebrate the birth of Christ was not in direct opposition to God's moral law—but other changes most decidedly were.

Roman Christians had already been distancing themselves

---

5. Most scholars are agreed that given the biblical evidence, Jesus could not have possibly been born in December—an unlikely time for shepherds to be out "keeping watch over their flock by night" (Luke 2:8).

from the Jews for hundreds of years, and in an empire where sun worship was highly fashionable (Constantine himself had been a sun worshiper), Christians began to naturally gravitate toward the weekly festival of the sun which was held on the first day of the week. (This is the reason that even today the first day of the week is called *Sun*day.) In A.D. 321, Constantine passed a law that effectively entrenched Sunday as the day of rest: "On the venerable Day of the Sun let the magistrates and people residing in cities rest, and let all workshops be closed. In the country, however, persons engaged in agriculture may freely and lawfully continue their pursuits; because it often happens that another day is not so suitable for grain-sowing or for vine-planting; lest by neglecting the proper moment for such operations the bounty of heaven should be lost."[6]

You will notice that the decree to observe Sunday as a day of rest was limited, at first, to those living in cities. There is some question whether or not Constantine actually intended this decree to support the Christian religion; he may have simply been entrenching an already popular pagan festival. Regardless of his motive, it was a hit with the Roman branch of Christianity, and as the Roman Church rose in prominence, it didn't take long for the practice to become universal. By the year A.D. 364, the Council of Laodicea officially rejected the Sabbath and enshrined Sunday worship as the universal practice for Christians: "Christians must not judaize by resting on the Sabbath, but must work on that day, rather honouring the Lord's Day; and, if they can, resting then as Christians. But if any shall be found to be judaizers, let them be anathema from Christ."[7]

It's important to remember that while Sunday worship and disregard for the Sabbath became the standard practice of Christians in the Roman Church (although Sabbath observance continued for

---

6. Codex Justinianus, lib. 3, tit. 12, 3; trans. in Philip Schaff, *History of the Christian Church,* 5th ed. (New York: Scribner, 1902), 3:380.

7. The Council of Laodicea, Canon 29.

centuries in other parts of Christendom), there was absolutely no biblical support for this custom. The declaration of the Council of Laodicea came hundreds of years after Christ returned to heaven and the last of the apostles had died. We should probably also ask why the Roman Christians felt it necessary to pass such a decree. It would be necessary only if a significant number of Christians were still keeping the seventh-day Sabbath at that time!

Who changed the Sabbath from Saturday to Sunday? *We* did it—the Christian church—without God's permission. Some years ago, I came across a remarkable little book by Peter Geiermann, *The Convert's Catechism of Catholic Doctrine.* If you've never been in a catechism class (I spent *years* in catechism classes), it is generally understood to be a doctrinal class in the Christian faith presented in question-and-answer format. Here's what I discovered in Mr. Geiermann's book:

> Q: Which is the Sabbath day?
> A: Saturday is the Sabbath day.
> Q: Why do we observe Sunday instead of Saturday?
> A: We observe Sunday instead of Saturday because the Catholic Church transferred the solemnity from Saturday to Sunday.[8]

There it is, in black and white. God didn't change the Sabbath. We did it. Here's another startling admission:

> The Bible still teaches that the Sabbath or Saturday should be kept holy. There is no authority in the New Testament for the substitution of Sunday for Saturday. Surely it is an important matter. It stands there in the Bible as one of the Ten Commandments of God. There is no authority in the Bible for abrogating this Command-

---

8. Peter Geiermann, C.SS.R., *The Convert's Catechism of Catholic Doctrine* (Rockford, Ill.: TAN Books, 1977), 50.

ment, or for transferring its observance to another day of the week. . . . The Church is above the Bible, and this transference of Sabbath observance is proof of that fact.[9]

The church is above the Bible? This is but a shadow of Lucifer, shaking his fist in the face of the Creator, saying, "No thank You, Sir, but I'll do things my *own* way!" There are human beings echoing a fallen angel: " ' "I will ascend above the heights of the clouds, / I will be like the Most High" ' " (Isaiah 14:14).

The sad truth is that we compromised. Christianity went through a long, terrible, dark period where we did things we ought to be deeply ashamed of. We persecuted, tortured, and killed those who didn't agree with us. We kept the Scriptures away from the general population, hidden in a language that most people didn't understand. And we came to the point that we found ourselves, in the footsteps of Lucifer, vying for the very throne of God.

Remember Paul's prediction that before the second coming of Christ there would be a great "falling away" (2 Thessalonians 2:3, 4)? And remember his concern that the "mystery of lawlessness" (2 Thessalonians 2:7) was already at work back in the early days of the Christian church? He was right on the money. Lucifer hates God's moral law and the Sabbath commandment in particular. He's been working overtime, trying to scrub the name of the Creator from human memory. And his crowning achievement is the fact that he managed to convince us to tamper with the Sabbath, God's permanent memorial to His goodness.

There's a stunning prophecy in the book of Daniel that warned us—thousands of years ago—that someone was going to tamper with God's moral code. It would, Daniel wrote, " ' "intend to change times and law" ' " (Daniel 7:25). You'd expect this to be an atheist or communist power to attempt such a feat. Who could have guessed that it would be *us*?

---

9. *The Catholic Record*, September 1, 1923, vol. XLV, no. 2342, 4.

Chapter Ten

A Few Important Details

When you first discover that the Sabbath has not been changed by God, but by human beings, a number of questions generally come to the forefront. In this chapter, we'll take a look at some of the most common questions people ask about the Sabbath.

1. How can we know which day is really the biblical seventh day? Hasn't the calendar been changed? What drives this question, of course, is the implication that if we can't know for sure which day is the biblical seventh day, then Sabbath observance is impossible. Of course, this would mean that God has placed an impossible requirement in His moral code and would support the devil's claims that God's government is unworkable and illegitimate.

If the calendar has become so confused that we can't know which day is the seventh day of the week, then that would also mean that we couldn't observe Sunday—the first day of the week—as a memorial of the Resurrection, either. We wouldn't know which day is the first day of the week.

Has the calendar been changed? The answer is Yes. But these changes have not altered the weekly cycle of days. In 1582, the Western world shifted from the Julian calendar to the Gregorian calendar, making an adjustment to correct an inaccuracy in the Julian calendar which didn't have the length of the day quite right. Ten days were dropped from the month of October so that in 1582, Thursday, October 4, was followed by Friday, October

15. Ten calendar *dates* were dropped, but Friday still followed Thursday, leaving the weekly cycle utterly unchanged.

Years ago, Bible scholar Francis D. Nichols sent a letter to the U.S. Naval Observatory, inquiring whether that organization knew of any historical disruption of the weekly cycle. The reply, dated March 12, 1932, and signed by Director James Robertson, stated, "There has been no change in our calendar in past centuries that has affected in any way the cycle of the week."[1]

That same year, Mr. Nichols also addressed his question to Sir Frank W. Dyson, Astronomer Royal of Great Britain. Sir Dyson replied, "As far as I know, in the various changes of the Calendar there has been no change in the seven day rota of the week, which has come down from very early times."[2]

The weekly cycle hasn't changed at all. In fact, in more than a hundred of the earth's languages, the seventh day of the week is still called "the Sabbath." The Spanish call it *sabado,* for example, and the Italians call it *sabbato.* In Arabic, it's *assabt.* In the Shona language of Zimbabwe, the seventh day is called *sabata.* There is overwhelming evidence that the seventh day of our calendar is still the Sabbath day.

2. Doesn't the Bible say, in Colossians 2:14–17, that the Sabbath has been abolished? Let's take a look and see what the text actually says: "having wiped out the handwriting of requirements that was against us, which was contrary to us. And He has taken it out of the way, having nailed it to the cross. Having disarmed principalities and powers, He made a public spectacle of them, triumphing over them in it. So let no one judge you in food or in drink, or regarding a festival or a new moon or sabbaths, which are a shadow of things to come, but the substance is of Christ" (Colossians 2:14–17).

There are a couple of issues we need to address in this passage,

1. Quoted in F. D. Nichols, *Answers to Objections* (Washington, D.C.: Review and Herald®, 1952), 560.

2. Ibid., 562.

because of a widespread misunderstanding in modern Christianity over what Paul is actually saying. To begin with, when Paul tell us that the "handwriting of requirements that was against us" was "nailed to the cross" by Christ, some people assume he means that the Ten Commandments were abolished at Christ's death. A little careful reflection reveals this suggestion is absurd. If the Ten Commandments have been abolished, that means *all ten of them are gone*—including the prohibitions against murdering and stealing! That obviously can't be true.

So what was nailed to the cross? We've already seen that God's moral law isn't *against* us; on the contrary, it's *for* God. It's a reflection of His perfect character, and to suggest that God's law is contrary to human beings would be the same as suggesting that God Himself is against the sinful human race. Even a quick glance through the Bible debunks this notion:

> For I know the thoughts that I think toward you, says the LORD, thoughts of peace and not of evil, to give you a future and a hope (Jeremiah 29:11).

> "For God so loved the world that He gave His only begotten Son, that whoever believes in Him should not perish but have everlasting life" (John 3:16).

When Paul talks about the "handwriting of requirements that was against us," he uses the Greek word *cheirographon*. Thayer's *Greek Lexicon* defines this word as "a note of hand, or writing in which one acknowledges that money has either been deposited with him or lent to him by another, to be returned at an appointed time." In other words, the *cheirographon* was a bill of debt, not a copy of the Ten Commandments. Paul is simply stating that Christ paid our debt of sin at the cross—which of course, was clearly *against* us.

The second issue we need to address in this passage has to do with Paul's counsel to "let no one judge you in food or in drink, or regarding a festival or a new moon or sabbaths, which are a shadow of things to come, but the substance is of Christ." Nowhere in this statement does Paul even remotely suggest that the Sabbath has been abolished or changed—he simply speaks about judging each other.

Closer examination of the passage reveals something else: Paul isn't even discussing the seventh-day Sabbath! In addition to the weekly Sabbath of the Ten Commandments, the Israelites observed a number of ceremonial sabbaths in connection with the sacrificial system. These included such annual festivals as the Passover and the Day of Atonement, which could fall on any day of the week, much the way your birthday or Christmas always come on the same *date* but on a different day of the week each year.

The word *sabbath* simply means "rest," and the Israelites rested— or "sabbathed"—both on God's weekly Sabbath and on these annual festivals. Note this example from the book of Leviticus: " ' "Also on the fifteenth day of the seventh month, when you have gathered in the fruit of the land, you shall keep the feast of the LORD for seven days; on the first day there shall be a sabbath-rest, and on the eighth day a sabbath-rest" ' " (Leviticus 23:39). Each of the annual festivals foreshadowed the work of Christ. (The Passover, for example, prefigured the death of Christ at the cross.) They also involved sacrifices, including meat and drink offerings (see Leviticus 23:37). They were clearly a part of the sacrificial system which *was* made redundant by the crucifixion of Christ. Note this observation made by the author of the book of Hebrews: "For the law, having a shadow of the good things to come, and not the very image of the things, can never with these same sacrifices, which they offer continually year by year, make those who approach perfect" (Hebrews 10:1).

This important passage identifies a law that regulates sacrifices that are offered "year by year," which of course, is the *ceremonial* law, not the Ten Commandments. It also calls it a "shadow of good things to come," the same language used by Paul to describe the sabbaths he identifies in Colossians 2:17.

What is Paul talking about? The sacrificial system, which also had "sabbaths." This is not a discussion of the seventh-day Sabbath!

3. What about Paul's declaration in Romans 14:5, 6 that it's up to the individual whether he or she keeps the Sabbath? Of course, it's always up to the individual whether he is going to keep the Sabbath, because God doesn't force people to obey. We have been given the right to choose—and the right to live with the consequences of our choices. That having been said, we should probably examine the passage in question: "One person esteems one day above another; another esteems every day alike. Let each be fully convinced in his own mind. He who observes the day, observes it to the Lord; and he who does not observe the day, to the Lord he does not observe it. He who eats, eats to the Lord, for he gives God thanks; and he who does not eat, to the Lord he does not eat, and gives God thanks" (Romans 14:5, 6). Context is all-important when it comes to understanding the Bible. Notice that Paul makes absolutely no mention of the Sabbath in this passage. He simply mentions a *day.* If we want to know what day he's talking about, we have to refer to the context. At the beginning of the chapter, Paul establishes an important point for understanding what he is saying: "Receive one who is weak in the faith, but not to disputes over doubtful things. For one believes he may eat all things, but he who is weak eats only vegetables. Let not him who eats despise him who does not eat, and let not him who does not eat judge him who eats; for God has received him" (verses 1–3).

First, Paul tells us that he is addressing a dispute "over doubtful things." Was there any doubt—whatsoever—regarding the seventh-day Sabbath? Absolutely not. It was firmly entrenched in God's moral law and had been a part of the life of God's people since the beginning of time.

Second, Paul raises the issue of eating—and not eating—

• 100 •

certain things. This is echoed later on in the passage when he says "He who eats, eats to the Lord . . . and he who does not eat, to the Lord he does not eat" (verse 6).

The key disputes that erupted in the early Christian church were not over the matter of keeping (or not keeping) God's moral law. They had to do with a different set of issues. In 1 Corinthians 8, for example, Paul addresses the issue of whether it was appropriate to eat food that had been offered to idols. Although idol worship is clearly prohibited by God's moral law, the Ten Commandments are silent on whether eating food that had been offered to an idol is in fact a form of worship. Some Christians felt that to eat the food was to acknowledge the idol, while others felt that since an idol was irrelevant and powerless, eating the food only underscored the fact that they did *not* honor it. Paul counseled them that they should be careful about each other's feelings in this matter, but he left it up to the individual to decide.

In Romans 14, Paul is addressing the issue of ritualistic eating practices and the special days associated with them. Were there special days in existence during which eating—or abstinence from eating—was practiced by the Jews? Absolutely. But the *Sabbath* is never mentioned, because it isn't Paul's topic. The context makes his subject clear: it has to do with *eating,* which is never mentioned in the fourth commandment. Paul is simply instructing believers that if they chose to continue observing fast days and feast days, it was up to them. But, again, he advises that they should be careful about each other's feelings (see Romans 14:13).

4. But isn't Sabbath keeping legalistic? That depends entirely on a person's reason for keeping the Sabbath! *Legalism* is a word that Christians throw around far too freely in an attempt to discredit each other. As it is commonly understood, *legalists* are people who are more concerned about the nitpicky details of something than they are about the spiritual meaning behind an observance. Jesus identified this problem among the Pharisees: " 'Woe to you, scribes and Pharisees, hypocrites! For you pay tithe of mint and anise and cummin, and have neglected the weightier matters of the law: justice and mercy and faith. These you ought to have done, without leaving the others undone. Blind guides, who strain out a gnat and swallow a camel!' " (Matthew 23:23, 24).

The Pharisees were very careful about tithing, but they weren't concerned at all about the things that matter most to God. As a result, they were merely going through the motions, and their religion was nothing but a formality. You'll notice, for the record, that as Jesus corrects them, He doesn't say that the details aren't important; He simply tells them they've lost the *meaning* of their religion.

Also, legalists are people who are trying to *earn* their salvation through their works.

Obviously, both of these characteristics of legalism signal an unhealthy approach to a relationship with God. If it's all about the details, and you ignore the very character of God, you're off base. If you're more worried about punching the clock when the sun goes down Friday than you are about having an intimate relationship with the God of the Sabbath, you've missed the point. It's not that observing the Sabbath according to God's instructions isn't important—it is. But without the relationship, it's just a formality!

Likewise, if you're keeping the Sabbath in order to score points with God, forget it. You simply cannot perform enough good deeds to purchase a spot in the kingdom of heaven—period! Christians don't keep the Sabbath in order to *be* saved. We keep it because we *are* saved. Jesus summed it up very nicely in John 14:15: " 'If you love Me, keep My commandments.' "

It is no more legalistic to keep the Sabbath than it is to refuse to take God's name in vain or refrain from murdering. Christians live in harmony with the Ten Commandments because they know it pleases God, and they love Him. Ask yourself this one question: would Adam and Eve have kept the Sabbath to earn salvation? Of course not. They didn't need salvation before the Fall, and the Sabbath was already in existence before sin came into the world!

The Sabbath is a matter of *loyalty*. God's people—particularly in the last days—have the Father's name written in their minds. Their hearts belong to Him entirely, and Sabbath observance serves as a public witness to this fact. The Sabbath is also a matter of recognizing your *relationship* with God: " ' "I am the LORD your God: Walk in My statutes, keep My judgments, and do them; hallow My Sabbaths, and they will be a sign between Me and you, that you may know that I am the LORD your God" ' " (Ezekiel 20:19, 20).

5. Didn't Jesus break the Sabbath? Preposterous! Jesus Himself said, " 'I have kept My Father's commandments and abide in His love' " (John 15:10). Matthew records Him as saying: " 'Do not think that I came to destroy the Law or the Prophets. I did not come to destroy but to fulfill. For assuredly, I say to you, till heaven and earth pass away, one jot or one tittle will by no means pass from the law till all is fulfilled. Whoever therefore breaks one of the least of these commandments, and teaches men so, shall be called least in the kingdom of heaven; but whoever does and teaches them, he shall be called great in the kingdom of heaven' " (Matthew 5:17–19). What are the odds that the sinless Son of God would say this and then proceed to break the commandments Himself? The idea that Jesus broke the Sabbath is based on a radical misunderstanding of the story in Matthew 12 when Jesus and His disciples picked grain to eat as they walked through a field on the Sabbath. They weren't bringing in the harvest; they were simply having a meal!

The Pharisees objected strenuously, suggesting that picking heads of grain was forbidden during the Sabbath hours. They also objected to the fact that Jesus healed a man on the same day. Truth be known, the Pharisees had added hundreds of human laws to the Sabbath in an effort to keep anyone from even getting *close* to breaking it. Spitting was forbidden, for example, because you might accidentally irrigate the grass and become guilty of farm labor. In the story under consideration, Jesus strips away the man-made burdens that had been added to the Sabbath. Read it carefully—He's not *breaking* the Sabbath; He's clarifying and restoring it!

6. *But what exactly do you do on the Sabbath?* Unfortunately, some of the fiery sermons bequeathed to us by Puritan preachers have given us the wrong impression about what God intends for us to enjoy on the Sabbath. Many have been led to believe that the Sabbath hours are little more than a cruel drudgery during which we are meant to sit quietly waiting for the sun to set on Saturday night.

I'm happy to report that nothing could be further from the truth. There's nothing at all burdensome about the Sabbath hours; on the contrary, we have full permission from God to *quit working or worrying* and *start living*! It's an opportunity to recapture some of that special sense of wonder we used to have when we were kids.

Think about the way the world has sucked all the joy out of living. I can see it clearly when I'm driving down the freeway with my kids. After they're finished asking "How much farther?" they want to stick their hands out the window and make them rise and fall in the air currents like little airplanes. (Even as I wrote that, I could suddenly feel myself doing it!) To the adults in the car, it's a huge nuisance. The wind messes up their hair and blows important documents around the car. We've become desensitized to the majesty of a thunderstorm, because we've seen thousands of storms in satellite photos, and we've mentally reduced them to numbers— inches of rain and wind velocity. But watch some kids when the thunder rolls; they still hear the voice of God.

The Sabbath was designed as dedicated time with God. It's a celebration of His goodness in creation, and according to Paul (see Romans 1:20), you can't help but find Him in the things He's made. One of my favorite activities on the Sabbath is to head outside to a patch of wilderness and spend time with my family—and my God. It's amazing how much more clearly you can hear God speak when you put aside the hassles of life for a day and just quietly spend time with Him in the grand cathedral of creation. "Be still, and know that I am God" (Psalm 46:10).

I don't really want to give you a list of activities for the Sabbath, because that can quickly become the sort of nitpicky legalism the Pharisees loved to engage in. There are general principles in the Bible, however, that serve to guide us in making wise choices during the Sabbath hours. I'll list a few of them:

- *Put aside your secular work (see Exodus 20:8–11).* This is perhaps the clearest instruction we have for the Sabbath hours. The Sabbath is a time of utter freedom from our day-to-day jobs. As part of his punishment for sin, Adam was told he'd have to *work hard* for a living (see Genesis 3:17–19). For twenty-four hours a week we get sheer relief from the curse!

- *Worship with other believers.* Jesus went to church on Sabbath (see Luke 4:15, 16). In this modern age, it's become popular to suggest that Christians can "go it alone," that they don't need to be part of a church. That's clearly an unbiblical idea. Christ commissioned us to carry the gospel to the world (see Matthew 28:18–20), and we're told that every one of us is given a unique set of gifts to contribute to the effort (see 1 Corinthians 12:4–27). No one has the ability to go it alone! The Sabbath is a special time when believers from all walks of life can assemble together and worship God. It is, after all, a day dedicated especially to the worship of the Creator! You notice in Hebrews 10:24, 25 that the Bible doesn't simply *suggest* corporate worship; it *requires* it. Read through the experience of Israel, and you'll see they spent a lot of Sabbaths worshiping together.

- *Do selfless acts of good for others.* Jesus healed the sick on the Sabbath (see Matthew 12:10–12). Some have taken this example to an extreme, volunteering their time to build houses with Habitat for Humanity or mowing lawns for shut-ins on the Sabbath. These can hardly be described as sacred activities in which the thoughts are on God or the salvation of others. An encouraging visit to a shut-in, however, in which you share the promises of God, a word of encouragement, and a prayer certainly fit the bill.

- *Spend time with your family.* Don't forget that marriage is also a God-given gift from Eden. (More on that in the next chapter.) Gather your family in the sanctuary of your home—or nature—and worship God.

- *Get out and enjoy the wonders of creation.* As previously mentioned, you'll find scores of lessons about your God there—and opportunities to hear His voice.

- *Rest!* This is a no-brainer. It's clearly one of God's intentions for the Sabbath (see Genesis 2:2, 3; Exodus 20:8–11). There's nothing quite as satisfying as a Sabbath nap, knowing that you're not even *allowed* to worry for the time being.

Again, I don't want to be prescriptive. You need to study biblical principles and build your Sabbath time with God yourself. I guarantee that if you spend it the way God intended, you'll never run out of things to do. In fact, you'll be surprised at how fast the Sabbath hours pass.

Chapter Eleven

A Monument in Time

"*Daddy!* What color comes next?" I heard the question only because my daughter's persistent tapping on my left shoulder prompted me to pull out one of my earphones. We were on a very full flight from Cincinnati to Los Angeles, and as always, I was blocking out the unwanted noise of the cattle-class cabin by blissfully immersing myself in Rachmaninoff.

"What was that, kiddo? I didn't hear you."

"What color comes next?" She was pointing at a sheet of paper on her tray table. It was a page that had been carefully torn from a coloring book, covered with typical little girl stuff—rainbows, shooting stars with hearts on them, and clouds (which were also emblazoned with hearts). The only thing missing from the picture to make it truly sickeningly sweet was a bunch of teddy bears. With her five-year-old finger pressed against an uncolored stripe on a rainbow, Naomi awaited my answer.

"It's *blue*, kiddo. Blue comes next."

"Thank you, Daddy!" She pulled her finger back off the page and methodically dug around in a small denim purse full of mismatched crayons until she found a blue one. Then, very carefully (in fact, much more carefully than you would expect from a five-year-old), she filled in the next stripe.

A few moments later, she was tapping my shoulder again. I should have predicted it would happen, but I didn't. I pulled out my earphone again.

The Sign

"*Then* what, Daddy? What comes next?" I glanced over at the page; there was only one stripe left. Apparently, the artists at the coloring book factory aren't paid enough, because they had drawn only five stripes in a rainbow that's supposed to have seven—as everybody knows. The next color after blue, of course, would have been indigo, but how do you explain indigo to a little kid? (Besides, I have a little trouble telling the various shades of purple apart myself.)

"It's *purple*," I said, feeling a little guilty about taking the easy way out—but with only one stripe left, what was I to do? Naomi pulled her bag of crayons up to her chin, flooding it with light from the overhead reading lamp. She turned and looked at me pleadingly.

"I don't think I have a purple crayon. Can you please help me find one, Daddy?"

I pushed the pause button on my iPod and pulled out my other earphone so I could devote my full attention to the task at hand. I dug around in her little cloth bag until I found something that looked purplish. The reading light, however, must not have had a full-spectrum bulb, because the crayon I extracted from the bag was, in fact, not purple. It was black!

It didn't end in artistic disaster, however, because Naomi tested it on the margin of the page before she applied it to the rainbow. "Daddy, this one's not purple!" She was a little indignant that I had been so unhelpful.

That's when I noticed that she had been testing *every* crayon before using it. There was a long series of careful crayon marks all the way down the left side of the page. I was amazed. Was this really *my* daughter being so careful? The one who never—*ever*—cleans her room and is quite happy to leave her station in the bathroom looking like Russian spies had been hastily looking for a hidden microfilm?

I stopped what I was doing (it was work, anyhow) and gave her my full attention. I watched as she diligently searched through the pencil case until she found a suitable replacement for my black crayon. Then she filled in the last stripe very carefully, with a determined expression on her face. Her tongue slipped out of the corner of her mouth—for just a moment—as she concentrated, a trait that has passed down through several generations on my mother's side. I've been caught doing it once or twice myself. As I watched the pint-sized artist sitting next to me, I suddenly imagined Van Gogh or Michelangelo doing the same thing as they agonized over minor imperfections in their masterpieces.

When the last stripe of the rainbow had been meticulously filled in, she stopped and inspected her work. Then she pointed to the top stripe. "Daddy, this one at the top isn't *really* red, but I don't have a red crayon. I tried to make it close, though. It's *close,* right?" Her index finger pressed against the top stripe of the rainbow hard enough to whiten her top knuckle.

It *was* close, so I reassured her. "It looks *great,* honey!" Why was she so worried? It was just another coloring page out of the hundreds she'd carelessly tossed on her bedroom floor or left outside in the rain. Who cared how close the colors were?

A look of concern spread across her face, and she held it up so I could inspect it more closely. "But do you think Mommy will like it?"

The truth be told, my kids could pretty much present my wife with a wad of used chewing gum sculpted into the shape of a heart, and she'd be thrilled as long as they said, "I love you, Mommy!" Pleasing their mother isn't that hard.

"I'm pretty sure she'll love it!"

The look of concern gave way to a contented smile. "Oh good!" she said, putting the picture down. "I'm going to wrap it up and give it to her for Christmas!" She carefully folded it over and then quickly turned and kissed my arm. "I love you, Daddy. A *lot!*"

I read somewhere that it costs more than four hundred thousand dollars to raise a child. If you ask me, that's a bargain. I'd pay double that amount for moments like that one, because for half a second the curtains of the universe were suddenly pulled back and I caught a glimpse of God. Sometimes, He has a way of showing up when you least expect it. Theologians have argued for centuries over what it means to be created in God's image, but in the airplane, I actually got to *see* what it means. He was there, in my daughter's drive to be creative. He was present in her determination to make her creation beautiful. I could see Him in her selfless, eager desire to make someone else happy.

God's fingerprints are all over my kids. For that matter, His fingerprints are pretty much everywhere. In spite of the way our rebellion has ruined His creation, you can still see Him in the things He has made.

> The heavens declare the glory of God;
> And the firmament shows His handiwork.
> Day unto day utters speech,
> And night unto night reveals knowledge.
> There is no speech nor language
> Where their voice is not heard.
> Their line has gone out through all the earth,
> And their words to the end of the world.
>
> In them He has set a tabernacle for the sun,
> Which is like a bridegroom coming out of his chamber,
> And rejoices like a strong man to run its race.
> Its rising is from one end of heaven,
> And its circuit to the other end;
> And there is nothing hidden from its heat (Psalm 19:1–6).

There's a reason that what's left of the original majesty of creation stirs up such incredible feelings in our hearts. Why is it that we can't seem to pull our eyes away from a sunset until the last dying embers of daylight finally sink below the horizon? Why is it that we never seem to get tired of looking at a palatial range of mountains capped with snow or of bathing in the shafts of orange and pink evening sunlight as they spill through the trees onto the forest floor? A simple tree, whose wonderful asymmetry stands in contrast to most human architectural designs, draws a lingering look from our eye while we sit shackled to a desk on the other side of an office window.

God must have been beside Himself with excitement when He designed this place. Go back to the Bible and notice some of the fine details of the Creation story. At the moment of creation, the angels simply couldn't contain themselves. They exploded with joy. " 'The morning stars sang together, / And all the sons of God shouted for joy' " (Job 38:7).

Watch God as He creates. At the end of each day, He steps back from His work and smiles. It is good! Not many people imagine God smiling anymore, because they've been given the impression—by a well-meaning but careless parent, a stern teacher, a clumsy sermon—that God is a joyless, severe Being whose sole purpose is to crack down on our fun. But apply a little reason to the biblical evidence. What are the odds that the angels were busy shouting for joy while God Himself slaved away with a furrowed brow and an angry frown?

"Then God saw everything that He had made, and indeed it was very good" (Genesis 1:31). God was deeply satisfied with what He had created. I sometimes imagine that it must have been a little like the satisfaction expectant parents feel when they finish decorating the nursery. Finally, everything is ready. It is time for the baby to arrive.

Try to imagine the moment God actually breathed life into Adam and woke him up. "Come on, Adam! Get up! There's so much to see!"

When our oldest daughter was still in a crib, I decided to sneak into her room one morning and steal a peek at her before she woke up. Honestly, there's nothing quite as heartwarming as watching your kids while they're sleeping. I swung the door open as quietly as I could, but to my disappointment, she was already awake.

At first, she kicked and gurgled a little, like most babies do when they see their parents. But then unexpectedly, she stopped moving, and her eyes grew wide with surprise. *What is so fascinating?* I wondered. Suddenly I realized what had happened. I had been brushing my teeth when I decided to sneak into her room, and my toothbrush was still hanging out of the corner of my mouth. Natalie had seen her daddy many times before, but not quite like this. In fact, she had never seen anyone brush their teeth—she didn't have any!

Strangely, I found myself a little jealous. Here was a brand-new human being—with everything still ahead of her. Almost everything that happened to her each day was a first. Nothing was boring or routine, including a toothbrush! I decided to give her a show. She squealed with delight as I opened my mouth wide so she could see what was happening. I even allowed a little toothpaste to dribble down my chin. Spend all the money you want on recreational vehicles or European vacations—nothing is as satisfying as watching your kid kick and wiggle as you show her the world.

Just try to imagine God's deep satisfaction as He showed our first parents around the Garden. Absolutely everything was new to them. Once in a while, they'd pause to express their delight over how much thought God had put into their home. "You mean You made this for *us*?"

Many of those thoughtful details still show through the scars we've etched on the face of God's masterpiece. If our existence— as the evolutionists like to suggest—is really just about survival, we could have made it on one article of food, one shape, one size, one flavor. A monochrome world would have also sufficed, where everything was black and white. Yet the Bible reveals a God who loves variety. It tells us that "out of the ground the Lord God made every tree grow that is pleasant to the sight and good for food" (Genesis 2:9). In thousands of years, you wouldn't run out of things to try on this planet—new flavors, new sights, new experiences. Built for eternal joy and lasting satisfaction for both God and man, it was the ideal place to experience the ideal relationship with God.

Now try to imagine the first time God returned to His garden after we decided to turn our backs on Him. Lucifer had not only challenged God's right to sit on heaven's throne, he had also caused human beings, created in God's image, to question His word. Those He had created for eternal friendship were hiding in the bushes, experiencing something they were never supposed to know—abject terror. Sucked in by Lucifer's lies about the character of God, they were actually afraid of their Creator.

Of course, I wasn't there, but I've played out the scenario in my mind many times. I've tried to picture coming home at the end of the day to discover my kids are missing. After searching all over the house, I find them hiding in a closet. As I open the door, one of them screams in fear. *They're terrified of me!* Just imagining the possibility breaks my heart. God actually lived through the experience.

Forever perish the thought that God has somehow isolated Himself from the suffering in our universe. He has felt it more deeply than anyone else. He has lived through the rejection of one-third of heaven's angels, and He watched us sell ourselves into the clutches of a liar and murderer. Every year, parents around this planet become sick with worry when their kids go missing: *Who's got them?* God doesn't have to wonder; He *knows.* He knows who holds us captive in the terrible, terminal slavery of sin. He knows who's using us as mere pawns to bring disrepute on His government, willing to throw us on the trash heap of history should we prove less than useful. (You'll notice that Satan killed all of Job's family except his wife, presumably because he still needed her to make Job more miserable.)

It's got to be sickening to God.

With tears in His eyes, God walks into the Garden that

evening, calling Adam's name. "Adam, where are you?" We're often tempted to think of God in terms of the pagan gods of our ancestors, storming into the Garden with thunderbolts flying out of His fists. Search the Genesis account carefully. There are no thunderbolts. Swiftly, God implements His plan to save us.

So the LORD God said to the serpent:

"Because you have done this,
You are cursed more than all cattle,
And more than every beast of the field;
On your belly you shall go,
And you shall eat dust all the days of your life.
And I will put enmity
Between you and the woman,
And between your seed and her Seed;
He shall bruise your head,
And you shall bruise His heel" (Genesis 3:14, 15).

A line is drawn in the sand. If people wish to restore their relationship with the Creator, they can do it. They will become the "woman," a symbol God uses to describe His people.[1] They will be redeemed from the slavery of sin by the blood of One who will come from their own line—the Seed of the woman, the Lamb slain from the foundation of the world (see Revelation 13:8). The devil will be crushed by the sacrifice of Christ at the cross. "Then I heard a loud voice saying in heaven, 'Now salvation, and strength, and the kingdom of our God, and the power of His Christ have come, for the accuser of our brethren, who accused them before our God day and night, has been cast down' " (Revelation 12:10).

Those who wish to remain in the devil's custody, of course, will be free to do so. God will not force anyone back into His kingdom against his or her will.

---

1. See Jeremiah 6:2 and Ephesians 5:25.

From that moment, there will be only two groups of human beings on the planet. On one side will be those whose hearts belong to the Creator, those who have the Father's name written in their foreheads (see Revelation 14:1) and who "keep the commandments of God and the faith of Jesus" (verse 12). On the other side will be those who choose to indulge their sinful pride and follow in the footsteps of the fallen angel. They choose to divert the worship due to the Creator and present their allegiance to Lucifer. Tragically, because they are deceived, many of them fail to realize precisely what they are doing. Ultimately, "All who dwell on the earth will worship him, whose names have not been written in the Book of Life of the Lamb slain from the foundation of the world" (Revelation 13:8).

The human race—because of its decision to rebel—is removed from Paradise. Knowing what kind of suffering lies ahead for those who parade behind the dragon, God cannot allow them to eat from the tree of life and live forever. The misery would be unthinkable. You'll notice, however, that He doesn't slam the door on the Garden. "He placed cherubim at the east of the garden of Eden, and a flaming sword which turned every way, to guard the way to the tree of life" (Genesis 3:24).

For the time being, the path was closed, but it was *guarded,* because when the conflict is over and all the decisions are final, God plans to open His garden again:

> And he showed me a pure river of water of life, clear as crystal, proceeding from the throne of God and of the Lamb. In the middle of its street, and on either side of the river, was the tree of life, which bore twelve fruits, each tree yielding its fruit every month. The leaves of the tree were for the healing of the nations. And there shall be no more curse, but the throne of God and of the Lamb shall be in it, and His servants shall serve Him. They shall see His face, and His name shall be on their foreheads (Revelation 22:1–4).

Thus began the existence we now endure as we wait for Christ to come. It *had* to be tougher, for our own good. " 'Cursed is the ground for your sake,' " God said to Adam (Genesis 3:17). If we weren't kept busy making a living, Lucifer would be sure to drag us further down the sewer of sin. To this day, we seem to be most immune to temptation when we're encouraging the image of the Creator in our hearts by doing something constructive with our time. And to keep our hearts alive with hope, God leaves His fingerprints everywhere.

Two specific gifts from God have survived the Fall, both of which were designed to draw us closer to God. One of them is the institution of marriage, which happens to be—in addition to the Sabbath—another thing that Lucifer seems desperate to annihilate. You're likely familiar with the grim statistics: 50 percent of first marriages end in divorce court. (Some studies put it as low as 41 percent—still a tragic figure.) Sixty-seven percent of second marriages and 74 percent of third marriages also collapse.[2] Today, vast numbers of children grow up entirely confused about what a family is supposed to look like.

Why do so many marriages fail? Is it because people don't want them to work? Or is something else at play? The relentless pressures of the modern, noisy world have made family life difficult for most and seemingly impossible for some. What is it about marriage that fallen angels don't want you to see? Paul pulls the mask off the devil's scheme in his letter to the Ephesians. Read it very carefully:

> Husbands, love your wives, just as Christ also loved the church and gave Himself for her, that He might sanctify and cleanse her with the washing of water by the word, that He might present her to Himself a glorious church, not having spot or wrinkle or any such thing, but

---

2. According to Jennifer Baker of the Forest Institute of Professional Psychology. See www.divorcerate.org/.

that she should be holy and without blemish. So husbands ought to love their own wives as their own bodies; he who loves his wife loves himself. For no one ever hated his own flesh, but nourishes and cherishes it, just as the Lord does the church. For we are members of His body, of His flesh and of His bones. "For this reason a man shall leave his father and mother and be joined to his wife, and the two shall become one flesh." This is a great mystery, but I speak concerning Christ and the church (Ephesians 5:25–32).

God created the institution of marriage to mirror our relationship with Him. In order to better help us understand how to relate to Him—and how tenderly He feels about us—He put human beings in a two-way relationship. Marriage is a microcosm, a school, for understanding the universe. Even after the Fall, it serves to show us what a healthy relationship with God is supposed to look like. Marriage helps re-create us in the image of Christ. Just like nothing is quite as satisfying as a healthy marriage, nothing is quite as fulfilling as knowing God intimately. It's no wonder the forces of darkness work overtime to put untold stress on human marriages. If we built them and managed them as God intended, we'd walk straight back into the arms of our Creator.

In addition to marriage, the Sabbath also survived our fall from grace. As we discussed near the beginning of this book, the Sabbath was originally intended as a memorial of God's creative power and love. After the Fall, it took on an added meaning. It stands as a pledge from God that He will re-create what we have thrown away. Just as the Israelites remembered their deliverance from slavery on the Sabbath (see Deuteronomy 5:15), so we continue to observe it in the knowledge that God is restoring in us the image of His Son and executing His plan to return us to Eden. We are, in Jesus Christ, a new creation (see 2 Corinthians 5:17).

At the end of every week, after facing the brutal realities of living in a sin-sick world, there is a monument in time to remind us that God has everything under control. Our world will not always be like this; God's going to fix it. There's not a thing Lucifer can do to remove God's monument. If God had chosen to hang a plaque on one of the trees in the Garden, someone could have ripped it down. If He had erected a tower to His name, someone could have knocked it over. But God saw to it that no one could destroy His sign—He built an unassailable monument in *time*.

"You're going to make it," God says. "In fact, one day you'll get to watch Me create a brand-new Paradise home for you. Count on it. Write it down. And every week, meet with Me so I can remind you of it."

Chapter Twelve

Following the Master

Before America dropped the atomic bomb on Hiroshima, the Halifax Explosion was the largest man-made explosion in the history of the world. The city of Halifax was a key Canadian port during the First World War, and the ongoing war in Europe made it a very busy place. Early in the morning of December 6, 1917, the unthinkable happened: two ships collided in the harbor. The worst part? One of them, the *Mont Blanc,* was loaded with tons of explosives, including two hundred tons of TNT, thirty-five tons of benzyl, and twenty-three hundred tons of picric acid. These explosives, originally destined for use against the Kaiser's troops, now became a threat at home. A shower of sparks created by the hulls of the ships rubbing against each other ignited the benzyl (which was stored on the open deck of the *Mont Blanc*), and panicky sailors immediately took to the lifeboats, rowing away as fast as possible.

Meanwhile, the sight of a large burning ship drew the attention of the citizens of Halifax. They couldn't hear the warning screams of the escaping sailors, so many of them laid aside their work and gathered on the shore to watch the spectacle, blithely unaware of the potential for disaster. Unmanned, the furiously burning ship drifted against a pier, setting it ablaze. At that point, the fire department was called in, and just as firemen were preparing to fight the flames, the *Mont Blanc* suddenly exploded. It would probably be more accurate to say it vanished! More than three hundred acres of the city were instantaneously destroyed. The blast leveled the city, and then a moment later, the vacuum created by the explosion sucked all the debris back into the devastated area, raining untold amounts of debris on the victims. To this day, you can see a piece of the ship's anchor, weighing eleven hundred pounds, that was dropped more than two miles from the harbor! Sixteen hundred people were killed in a couple of seconds; nine thousand more received serious injuries. One of the most common injuries? *Broken glass lodged in the eye.* So many people, you see, had been standing at their windows watching the ship burn.

Consider this story for a moment. When fire erupted on the *Mont Blanc,* most of the people on shore were irresistibly drawn to the sight. Now imagine Eve, transfixed by a talking serpent. She had already been warned to stay away from this particular tree, but in a perfect world where humans were innocent, how could she possibly comprehend the potential for misery and suffering? She had never witnessed death. Ignoring all the warnings, she stayed—and then the situation exploded. The shards of rebellion pierced the human soul, and God wept.

Dorothy Swetnam-Hare survived the Halifax Explosion. On the fateful morning of December 6, she was sitting in a rocking chair, listening to her mother practice the piano in the living room. Her father and brother were also home. At about five minutes after nine o'clock, the house suddenly collapsed without warning. Dorothy, only six years old at the time, found herself trapped under a mountain of broken beams and shattered plaster.

It was quiet for a moment, and then she heard her father's voice. "Lizzy? Carmen?" There was no answer from either her mother or brother; they had not survived. In the dark, dusty rubble of her home, she called out, "Where are you, Daddy?"

It didn't take him long to find her. "Dot," he called, "you've got to allow yourself to be pulled out of this hole, no matter how much it hurts."

Step back from your life for a moment and take stock of

what's happened so far. Life on a ruined planet is hard. Most of us are still walking around with the shards of sin blinding our eyes, unable to see what has caused all the pain. The devil, of course, is delighted to keep us in that condition, for fear that the truth will get out and we will discover him to be a liar and a murderer. In the words of the apostle Paul: "If our gospel is veiled, it is veiled to those who are perishing, whose minds the god of this age has blinded, who do not believe, lest the light of the gospel of the glory of Christ, who is the image of God, should shine on them" (2 Corinthians 4:3, 4).

But somewhere in our hearts is a memory of our Father, for He has planted eternity in our hearts. He has not left Himself without witness. From underneath the rubble of our sin-blasted world, we can hear Him searching for His missing family, calling them by name. " ' "Behold," ' " says Jesus, " ' "I stand at the door and knock. If anyone hears My voice and opens the door, I will come in to him and dine with him, and he with Me" ' " (Revelation 3:20).

Desperate for help—desperate to understand our plight and find meaning in our lives—we cry out, "Where are You, Father?" Moments later, He is there, reaching through the rubble to save us. "OK," He says, "hang on to Me. You've got to let Me pull you out of this hole, no matter how much it hurts."

There's a reason Jesus calls the gate to heaven "narrow" and the road to the kingdom "difficult" (see Matthew 7:14). God has to make changes in our hearts if we're going to be ready for the kingdom, and like when a dangerous tumor is being carefully excised from our body, the experience can be a little painful. " ' "I counsel you," ' " says Jesus, " ' "to buy from Me gold refined in the fire, that you may be rich; and white garments, that you may be clothed, that the shame of your nakedness may not be revealed; and anoint your eyes with eye salve, that you may see" ' " (Revelation 3:18). Fire hurts, but it also purifies and cleanses.

One influential young ruler missed the kingdom by a mere moment. When he realized that escaping the wreckage of this planet and inheriting eternal life would mean that he had to give up what he treasured most in life, he shied away from the Surgeon's scalpel. " 'Go your way,' " Jesus told him, " 'sell whatever you have and give to the poor, and you will have treasure in heaven; and come, take up the cross, and follow Me' " (Mark 10:21).

A cross? He couldn't do it. His problem wasn't really the money. Even though many people would love to believe that affluence automatically bars a person from the kingdom of heaven, Jesus makes it plain that this wasn't the real problem. When Jesus uttered that famous statement, " 'It is easier for a camel to go through the eye of a needle than for a rich man to enter the kingdom of God' " (verse 25), the disciples reacted with horror. " 'Who then can be saved?' " they asked (verse 26).

The disciples were not, as far as we know, wealthy men. After the young man left, they struggled to understand how anyone could possibly be saved. It clearly wasn't the money. It was a much more fundamental issue: this young man couldn't let go of this world and simply surrender *completely* to Jesus. "You've got to let Me pull you out of the wreckage, no matter how much it hurts," God says.

"I can't do that," the young man replied.

Salvation takes utter and complete surrender. It is not a matter of how clever or resourceful you are. It does not depend on what you can do for God; it hinges on what He can do for you. Are you willing to place yourself in His hands? Are you willing to let Him pull you out of the wreckage because you *can't* do it yourself?

The weekly Sabbath is a potent symbol of surrender. Every week, when the sun sets on Friday evening, God invites you to enter into His rest. Your work might not be finished; your worries might not be resolved. It requires *surrender.* Can you really do it? Can you stop obsessing about life and leave things to God for twenty-four hours? Can you set everything aside and just *rest* in God?

It's an act of faith. It's a step toward the Creator, a declaration that your life is utterly in His hands and that You trust Him to take care of things. On the Sabbath, we close our eyes and fall backward into His waiting arms—and He catches us.

Even though the disciples were technically keeping the Sabbath the night Jesus was murdered, they weren't really keeping it—at least not the way that God intended. Understandably, they were worried. By all appearances, the kingdom of God had suffered an irreversible blow. Jesus, after all, was dead—and who knew whether or not the authorities were pounding the pavement looking for them? Who would be the next to hang on a cross?

They may have laid aside their temporal work, but in their hearts, they weren't really observing the Sabbath. When Jesus found them on the first day of the week, they were huddled together, hiding. Forgetting His promise that He would rise from the dead, they were gathered in "fear of the Jews" (John 20:19). One of Jesus' followers had fled the scene of the Master's arrest. Another had actually denied knowing Him at all. The Bible mentions only John and the women at the cross. Chances are, they didn't observe the Sabbath that week the way God intended.

"You've got to hang on to Me and let Me pull you out," God says. "Depend on Me. Lean on Me completely." In the book of Ezekiel, God says, " 'Moreover I also gave them My Sabbaths, to be a sign between them and Me, that they might know that I am the LORD who sanctifies them' " (Ezekiel 20:12).

Some people have suggested that keeping the Sabbath is a form of salvation by works. They couldn't be more wrong. The Sabbath is about *surrender.*

When search parties came to Dorothy's house, there was almost nothing left. One of the few things to survive the disaster is on display at the Maritime Museum in Halifax. It's a simple shaving mug, with the words, "Remember Me," painted on the side. Every week, God says the same thing—" 'Remember the Sabbath day, to keep it holy' " (Exodus 20:8). It's an invitation, in the wreckage of our ruined world, to remember our Creator and plant a flag of faith that says we trust Him with our future.

Epilogue

It's a Friday night at the Boonstra household, and outside our living room window, the sun is setting. The house is spotless (most of the time), and my family is gathered around the coffee table in the family room. Most nights, my wife insists that we eat at the kitchen table, but this night is different. It's the Sabbath.

I look at my two daughters who have looked forward to this moment all week. They have never known anything different, although I didn't discover the wonders of the Sabbath until I was an adult. I've heard people say that Sabbath keeping is burdensome, but that's a little like saying that enjoying Thanksgiving is a form of spiritual bondage. I'm not sure where such individuals get the idea that the Sabbath is a prison for legalistic people; apparently, they've never really experienced it.

Borrowing an idea from our Jewish friends, we've placed two candles on the table. Each of my girls takes a turn lighting one, and they explain what the flame represents. "This candle calls us to *remember* the seventh day, to keep it holy," one of them says. "And this one calls us to *observe* the Sabbath," replies the other. Now their eyes are sparkling with candlelight, and we open a children's story Bible and share a story together. At the close of the story, we all kneel for prayer, and I specifically ask God for a blessing for my kids. Then we eat. It's a simple meal, but always excellent. We share a bottle of the very best grape juice we can lay our hands on, and long into the evening we talk. I ask my children what they think about God and answer their questions.

I've got to say—it's pretty nice.

Outside our door, the world continues to worry about its problems and beats its fists against the air. But for right now, for an entire twenty-four hours, we can leave that behind. We can rest in the arms of our God, knowing that He loves us and that we are secure in Jesus Christ. For a moment, we get to visit Eden and catch a glimpse of what God intended for families to enjoy in His presence. The only way the forces of evil can touch us in this moment is if we allow them in. It's a little taste of heaven, a down payment on the world to come.

The first time God created this planet, we weren't there to see it. Angels saw it, but not human beings. God didn't breathe life into Adam until the last part of the sixth day. Did God wait until the end of Creation week so that Adam's first experience would be the Sabbath—an intimate moment with his Creator? Did His eyes sparkle with delight as the sun set that night and His new friendship with us began?

We weren't there to see Him create our world the first time, but I strongly suspect we'll see Him do it the next time around. Listen carefully as He speaks:

> "For behold, I create new heavens and a new earth;
> And the former shall not be remembered or come to
>   mind.
> But be glad and rejoice forever in what I create;
> For behold, I create Jerusalem as a rejoicing,
> And her people a joy.
> I will rejoice in Jerusalem,
> And joy in My people;
> The voice of weeping shall no longer be heard in her,
> Nor the voice of crying" (Isaiah 65:17–19).

Can you hear it? Can you hear the eager sense of anticipation in the Creator's voice? "Don't worry," He says, "I'm going to turn it all around." I like the fact that He starts with the word *behold*. That's the kind of dramatic thing you say when you want somebody to *see* something. Once it's all over, and we're safely home, I'm guessing Jesus will light up with glee and say, "Over here, everybody. *Watch this!*" And then He does it again—He speaks our world into existence. It will be a much different place than we're used to:

> And I saw a new heaven and a new earth, for the first heaven and the first earth had passed away. Also there was no more sea. Then I, John, saw the holy city, New Jerusalem, coming down out of heaven from God, prepared as a bride adorned for her husband. And I heard a loud voice from heaven saying, "Behold, the tabernacle of God is with men, and He will dwell with them, and they shall be His people, and God Himself will be with them and be their God. And God will wipe away every tear from their eyes; there shall be no more death, nor sorrow, nor crying; and there shall be no more pain, for the former things have passed away." Then He who sat on the throne said, "Behold, I make all things new." And He said to me, "Write, for these words are true and faithful" (Revelation 21:1–5).

No more tears. No more pain. No more suffering. No more standing by the open grave of someone you've lost to the icy clutches of death. This time, no one is going to revolt. No one is going to question God's word, because we've seen—beyond all shadow of doubt—that He really *does* have our best interests at heart. We've also seen, firsthand, what rebellion did to our last home. Lucifer is gone (see Ezekiel 28:18, 19). The reckless challenge to God's throne has passed. We know who belongs on the throne, and amazingly, He invites us to sit with Him there:

" ' "To him who overcomes I will grant to sit with Me on My throne, as I also overcame and sat down with My Father on His throne. He who has an ear, let him hear what the Spirit says to the churches" ' " (Revelation 3:21, 22).

It's Friday night at the Boonstra home, and the candlelight dances in my children's eyes. It's a little taste of what's coming. I can't wait. God can't, either. "Write it down," He says, "for these words are true and faithful" (see Revelation 22:6).